THE SOFT SCIENCE OF TENNIS

Frank Giampaolo

TESTIMONIALS FROM THE INTERNATIONAL TENNIS INDUSTRY

"At crunch time, the athlete's inner dialog (self-coaching) makes all the difference. *The Soft Science of Tennis* explains how to override negative past belief systems and how to eliminate judgment in competition. This book of wisdom should be on every coach's and parent's bedside."

Stevie Johnson, *Manhattan Beach, California, #21 ATP Professional, Olympian, Most decorated NCAA player of all time*

"Brilliantly captivating and insightful. Frank Giampaolo is truly a 'Teacher's Teacher' – of all of his many incredible publications, *The Soft Science of Tennis* is one of his best, and will surely move the tennis teaching industry forward. Athletes will be celebrating greater degrees of happiness and confidence knowing that their trusted coaches truly understand their genetic design."

Dick Gould, *Palo Alto, California, Emeritus, Men's Tennis Coach, Director of Tennis, Stanford University Winner of 17 NCAA Men's Championships*

"*The Soft Science of Tennis* specializes in interpreting human behavior within the development of competitive athletes. I highly recommend it to parents and coaches."

Peter Smith, *Long Beach, California, USC Men's Tennis Coach, A five-time Pac-12 Coach of the Year and Two-Time ITA National Coach of the Year, 5- Time NCAA National Champion*

"Under pressure, we'd like to think that our athletes will rise to the occasion...they don't. They sink to the level of their physical, mental and emotional training. *The Soft Science of Tennis* delves deeper than strokes and uncovers how to get the most out of each individual."

Dr. Mark Kovacs, *Atlanta Georgia, Executive Director, International Tennis Performance Association (itpa-Tennis.org) CEO, Kovacs Institute (Kovacs institute.com)*

"Frank Giampaolo has a rich understanding of what it takes to be a successful tennis player. With passion and nuance, this book provides a great many insights -- especially in such more mysterious realms as emotion and character. There's a lot to be learned here."

Joel Drucker, *Writer for Tennis Channel and Historian-at-large for the International Tennis Hall of Fame*

"From my personal ATP experience, I can honestly say I struggled with the 'software' part most of my tennis career. Back then there was very little information on how to develop the 'mental or emotional muscles.' Frank has been doing this successfully for the past decade. I 1000% believe that the 'software' (mental & emotional) part of tennis is as important to build as the hardware (strokes & athleticism). I highly recommend Frank's latest book: *The Soft Science of Tennis*. It's an outstanding contribution to the game. If I had Frank coaching me...I would have won way more titles on tour."

Johan Kriek, *West Palm Beach, Florida. Former Top 5 ATP, 2-Time Grand Slam Champion, owner, Johan Kriek Tennis Academy*

"Frank Giampaolo has nailed it again in *The Soft Science of Tennis*. This time he has led us to see the absolutely critical importance of connecting with our students by understanding their personality profile, cognitive design and learning styles. All great teaching begins with the tools he provides. Thanks to Frank for giving them to us in this outstanding book."

Tim Mayotte, *Boston, Massachusetts, Former Top 7 ATP, NCAA Singles Champion, USTA National Coach*

"*The Soft Science of Tennis* is another valuable resource from Frank Giampaolo. He is knowledgeable and passionate about sharing – these two qualities demonstrate why Frank has been a top-rated presenter at the PTR International Tennis Symposium. In *The Soft Science of Tennis*, Frank gets the message across and reminds us what's truly important in our coaching. Communication, Engagement, Life Skills and Character Building are what really matter in the mark we leave on our students after we are gone!"

Julie Jilly, *Hilton Head, South Carolina, PTR VP Marketing/Events*

"Frank Giampaolo once again demonstrates that he is the supreme grand master of tennis psychology. What distinguishes champions from other players is what goes on inside their minds. If you want to play better and understand the kind of training is likely to work best for you, read this. Then, read it again."

Clinton W. McLemore, *Laguna Niguel, California Ph.D., Clinical Psychology, USC*

"Frank Giampaolo has done it again. His new book *THE SOFT SCIENCE OF TENNIS* is all about what REALLY matters in tennis. In a world where most players are on an endless pursuit to perfecting their strokes, Frank teaches players about the BIG picture... things that will matter in the long run. If you're serious about improving your game and thinking outside the box... this book is for you."

Jorge Capestany, *Michigan USPTA Master professional, PTR International Master professional, Founder, CapestanyTennis.com*

"Frank has hit another 'ace' with his latest book *The Soft Science of Tennis*. He is a wealth of information in so many areas of tennis and always does a fantastic job in addressing the needs of athletes, parents, and coaches. This book's an amazing read touching on the hidden topics of advanced communication and personality profiling which are often missed by many coaches."

Michele Krause, *Sarasota, Florida TIA Global Education Director- Cardio Tennis*

"Frank's positive attitude and his ability to see tennis from different angles make his insights fresh and unique. In *The Soft Science of Tennis*, Frank once again shows us different, powerful pathways to success."

Eliot Teltscher, *Irvine, California Top #6 ATP player, Former managing director of the USTA Player Development Program*

"*The Soft Side of Tennis* is filled with insight and inspiration to help you reach your potential. In this extraordinary book, Frank Giampaolo shows you how to successfully utilize your skill set by developing a positive mindset."

Roger Crawford, *Sacramento California, Host of Tennis Channel's Motivational Monday's, Best-Selling Author-Hall of Fame Speaker*

"*The Soft Science of Tennis* is not just another tool in your toolbox but another complete toolbox that every coach and parent should read. As in any sport, technical and physical abilities will not flourish until mental capabilities grow and strengthen. Frank takes you through the effective steps of how to assist your athletes in developing a strong and positive mindset. Any coach or parent trying to help a player who is striving for excellence, must read this book. This is definitely a book that I will purchase for the entire High-Performance coaching staff at CDL."

Dean Hollingworth, *Montreal, Quebec, Canada, WTA Trainer, CSCS, MTPS Director of High-Performance Club CDL*

"Great book! I believe this is going to help a lot of coaches and players. It should be part of the mandatory curriculum as a teaching professional. The four parts of a performance paradigm are physical, equipment, technical, and mental. This book is a must for the mental side of the athlete. If you're into building champions of life and on-court this book is a must."

Dr. Sean Drake, *Oceanside California, Performance Director at TPI*

ACKNOWLEDGMENT

Thank you to my friends at (PTR) Professional Tennis Registry especially Julie W. Jilly for the editing. I'm grateful for her expertise and kindness. Craig Cignarrelli for the friendship and his "off the charts" Tennis IQ. His opinions helped shape this book's content. To my new partners, Amy Wishingrad and the folks at Head/Penn. I'm forever indebted to the staff of The Vic Braden Tennis College and Coto Research Center for molding my soft skills.

A special thanks goes to my longtime friend Craig Tiley for offering to forward *The Soft Science of Tennis*.

As always, I'm deeply thankful to my partner Linda for her patience and support. Without her, this book would not have materialized.

Lastly, I'm honored by all the international tennis industry experts who put aside their busy schedule to write a testimonial quote for this book. My heartfelt gratitude goes out to each one of you.

CONTENTS

FOREWORD

Frank Giampaolo and I have been friends and colleagues since 1987 when we ran Vic Braden Tennis Colleges in Cape Cod Massachusetts. Frank has been a constant voice on the world's tennis stage with his International bestselling books and world speaking engagements.

The Soft Science of Tennis is quite possibly Frank's best work to date. It's a fast read with compelling strategies for developing the whole athlete. It is a must for those parents and coaches fixated solely on fundamental stroke production. Within this work, Frank digs deep into how and why profiling each athlete's inborn, cognitive design is the backbone of maximizing each individual's potential. In regards to the art of communication, this book contains everything coaches and parents need to know.

Within minutes of scrolling through the pages, the reader will surely be asking, "Why isn't everyone teaching this?" As expected, Frank is once again, thinking outside of the square and is one step ahead.

I am writing this foreword because this book matters. It will drastically change the way you think about the art and science of coaching the game of tennis. The Soft Science of Tennis is filled with sports psychology insights, emotional storytelling and, practical solutions to assist athletes, parents, and coaches on their journey.

Enjoy this ground-breaking read.

Craig Tiley
Chief Executive Officer of Tennis Australia and Australian Open Tournament Director.

PREFACE

During the past three decades, the business of tennis coaching has become much more scientific. Biomechanics, technique, and technology have changed the hardware (strokes and athleticism) for the better, yet, the software (mental and emotional) have been routinely ignored.

I was fortunate to begin my career at The Vic Braden Tennis College as a tennis instructor. Back in the 1980's stroke production was the focal point. As I opened and directed tennis colleges throughout the country, I had the opportunity to work with top nationally ranked athletes and touring pros. It was then that I realized that although stroke production was fundamental to the game of tennis, it was by no means the whole story. I found that the athletes with sound hardware (strokes and athleticism) and under-developed software (mental and emotional components) struggled in competition. So, for the past 20 years, I've immersed myself into the study of the athlete's competitive software.

When Sergey Brin and Larry Page founded Google in 1998, they believed that only techies understood technology, so they set the companies hiring algorithms to employ computer science students from elite Universities. Fifteen years later Google began Project Oxygen to test their hiring methods. The conclusion of the research project shocked everyone. Among the seven most valued qualities of Google's top employees, technical expertise came in dead last. Interestingly, what proved more important to their corporate culture were SOFT SKILLS.

The following are the seven essential personality traits Google prioritizes in their hiring process:

1) Effective Coaching Skills
2) Effective Communication and Listening Skills
3) Empathy and Support for Others
4) Effective Critical Thinking Skills
5) Effective Problem Solving Skills
6) Ability to Connect Across Complex Ideas
7) Technical Expertise

Since exposing these findings, Google takes soft skills very, very seriously.

Like Google's search engine business, most of the tennis teaching industry assumes that hard skills (biomechanics and tennis technical knowledge) are most important. This book intends to share insights as to why soft skills matter and their significance may be more important than we were led to believe. The beliefs of athletes are directly influenced by their interactions with coaches and parents. After all, great coaching requires great collaborating, which is at the heart of *The Soft Science of Tennis*.

This book is designed to improve our tennis specific soft skills that are the behaviors that enable us to connect more efficiently. Soft science characteristics are learned behaviors, and when properly nurtured lead to more effective and harmonious development of our athletes.

In the two years, it took me to research and write this book, the one reoccurring theme throughout this journey was "invest in the person, not just the player." Whatever industry your athletes choose, whichever position they desire, they'll take their soft skills with them for the rest of their life.

INTRODUCTION

Let's begin by using a computer analogy, if strokes and athleticism are the athlete's hardware, mental and emotional skills are surely the athlete's software.

We all know that mental toughness and emotional resolve are critical in competition. *The Soft Science of Tennis* is specially designed to improve the mysterious software skills. With this groundbreaking book, respect is developed, and trust is earned as coaches and parents create an exceptional culture, sharpen **stronger** communication techniques, and connect with each student at a much deeper level.

The Soft Science of Tennis identifies each athlete's individual personality profile and unique cerebral design. Throughout these pages, we'll expose how your athlete's inborn genetic predispositions affect their behavioral attributes and on-court competitive characteristics.

Getting into the student's world requires the open-mindedness to embrace how the student's genetic predispositions impact their match play.

"You must first get into their world to change their world."

This book challenges coaches, athletes, and parents to recognize that preferred learning styles and training requirements are unique to each athlete.

The science of profiling personality isn't new or even unique. Today there are dozens of profiling programs including Disc, Social styles, Predictive Index, Profiles Int., HBDI, Strengthfinder, Keirsey Temperament, TTI, Human Metrics, and MBTI to name a few. These models all share in helping us better connect and communicate. *The Soft Science of Tennis* applies the Myers Briggs Type Indicator because it is the most widely recognized profiling application in use around the world.

MBTI is a registered trademark, and inside this book, I am simply sharing my unique, tennis specific understandings of their application.

Brain design awareness enhances our ability to customize our teaching approach to the different personality profiles found in the sport. While there are many interpretations of personality profiling, *The Soft Science of Tennis* aims to share techniques that I've found highly successful in my 30 years of coaching tennis.

Also included is the importance of nurturing positive character traits and life skills, and why developing a healthy moral compass matters. This soft science book dissects how to conquer essential performance anxieties such as overriding negative belief systems, eliminating internal judgment and building coachable athletes.

"In the coaching field, there is more to the story than teaching fundamental strokes. An athlete's negative emotional state can and will derail great game plans and exquisite strokes."

Rounding out this book, are several chapters uniquely focused on how to change fixed mindsets, managing fear and risk, and developing confidence and self-esteem. These are some of the favorite topics of high IQ coaches attending my conferences around the world. Consequently the question, "Why doesn't anyone else teach this stuff?" has become a reoccurring theme of discussion among coaches and parents alike throughout my travels. Within these pages, it is my goal to share everything you didn't even know…you needed to know about the soft science of tennis.

CHAPTER 1: Creating an Exceptional Culture

Mr. Martinez is the tennis operations manager at Big Sky Country Club. A short time ago, he hired Richard as their new tennis director. Richard played college ball, graduated with a highly regarded tennis management degree and his resume checked all the boxes. On the technical side, Richard was microscopically detailed. He could spot a student's opposing force vectors on their serve six courts away. He was adept at video analysis, organizing compass draws, teaching stroke fundamentals and eager to oversee the clubs racket stringing service. On paper, Richard was a good fit for a Country Club.

Sadly, within weeks, Richard turned out to be a nightmare. While he had tennis business knowledge, he possessed no interpersonal communication skills. Richard's interactions with members and co-workers were so poor; it led to his termination just one month into the job. Let's look into why Richard was let go so soon from Big Sky Country Club.

Richard had a pompous demeanor toward everyone all the time. When adult members would ask for his assistance, he would respond with a loud, disrespectful sigh. When Mrs. Jones asked him to fill in with the ladies league for 15-20 minutes until Helen arrived, Richard shook his head in disgust and said, "My hitting rate is the same as my lesson rate. For me to go on court, it's $120.00 an hour!" Richard even drew complaints from the parents of the junior program because he would scold the children if they smiled and laughed in their beginner's clinic. Richard was a taskmaster, and to him, clinics were to work and not to play.

The clubs co-workers were also scared of Richard. His pessimistic problem-oriented view of his job made him uncomfortable to be around. The clubs assistant pros reported that he would consistently complain about the facility and the management staff directly to the members. His negative verbal and nonverbal communication reaped havoc throughout the club.

Richard was also incompetent at the most essential interpersonal communication skill: listening. For example, one Friday afternoon, Mr. Martinez, the club manager, handed two rackets to Richard and told him that he had assured junior club member, Joey, that both his rackets would be strung by Saturday morning at 8:00 am. He could pick them up on his way out-of-town to the tournament. Although Richard was looking at Mr. Martinez as he took Joey's rackets from him, Richard wasn't listening. His focus was on a tennis match on the pro-shop television.

So Joey and his dad stopped in Saturday morning, and his rackets sat unstrung in the pro-shop. The members were obviously upset, and Mr. Martinez was furious with Richard. Mr. Martinez addressed Richard about why they were not strung, and he snapped: "You didn't tell me to string them yesterday!"

After multiple "red flags," Mr. Martinez had no choice but to put Richard on probation. Richards's lack of interpersonal communication skills continued to disrupt the clubs optimistic culture. Richard didn't possess the ability to problem solve, adapt, correct issues or even care to attempt to fit into the clubs corporate guidelines. The final straw was when a member came into the pro-shop and complained that his children are no longer enjoying the clinics and they are considering going elsewhere for lessons. Richard took it personally, called the member an idiot, and instigated a shouting match, "If you want Mikey and Lauren to learn the correct strokes, let me do my job! If you want them to be hackers…then go! I don't care!"

Richard's lack of communication skills instigated his firing. He couldn't apply appropriate decision making, empathy, analyze options or come up with win-win solutions. It was his way or the highway- period. Insulting the members prompted Richard's demise. The members quit the club and Richard lost his job.

Interpersonal Communication

If technical knowledge is the **science** of teaching, interpersonal communication is the **art** of teaching. Interpersonal communication characterizes the interaction that takes place between two or more people. In the coaching world, gaining an understanding of the sports biomechanics is important, but mastering communication is essential. Is your athlete being nurtured interpersonal skills? The following is a laundry list of interpersonal communication skills that facilitate success in tennis and in life.

Accountable, Accuracy, Adaptability, Adept, Alertness, Ambition, Amiability, Analytical, Articulate, Assertive, Attentiveness, Business-like, Capable, Caring, Competence, Confidence, Conscientiousness, Considerate, Consistency, Cooperation, Creative, Critical Thinking, Dedication, Dependability, Detail Oriented, Determination, Diplomatic, Efficiency, Empathy, Encouraging, Energy, Enterprising, Ethical, Experienced, Flexibility, Hardworking, Helpfulness, Honesty, Imaginative, Independent, Industriousness, Influential, Innovation, Insightful, Intuitive, Leadership, Logical Thinking, Loyal, Management, Motivation, Nonverbal Communication, Optimism, Organizational, Passion, Patience, Perceptive, Positive, Practical, Problem Solving, Productive, Professional, Progressive, Punctual, Rational, Realistic, Reflective, Reliable, Resourceful, Respectful, Responsible, Sense Of Humor, Sincere, Sociable, Teachable, Teaching, Teamwork, Technical Literacy, Tolerance, Trustworthy, Understanding, Verbal Communication, Versatility, Visionary, Work Ethic…Whew!

Without a doubt, any parent or coach would love to have their athletes possess these personal skills.

Excellence begins with a positive culture both at home and at the club. In our sport, invested athletes don't search out places like "Allen's Average Tennis Academy" or "Mike's Mundane Monday Night Clinic." On a conscious level, parents and athletes seek excellent technical knowledge. On the subconscious level, they pursue meaningful interpersonal relationships.

The culture I recommend is solution-oriented versus problem-oriented. Athletes are much more likely to flourish in a solution orientated environment. Coaches that provide a solution-based program are teaching lasting life skills.

A Great Replacement Tip:

Occasionally trade in the old school, pre-hit stretching routine with an upbeat dance-off. Turn up the tunes and watch athletes laugh their guts out while they dynamically stretch their bodies. Trust me, even if they arrive tired, stressed or negative, as they let go, they'll dance their worries away, and you'll have 25 kids with 25 huge smiles!

A positive mindset is a precursor to a meaningful session. Parents, the preceding replacement solution also works wonders at home as a way to motivate the family to seek optimism.

"An exceptional culture creates the positive attitude and mindset that promotes growth strategies, which in turn sustains excellence in competition."

It's important to note that despite the student's inherent athletic ability, level of play or commitment to the game, each student deserves the same sports science data, focus, and energy as a high performer. In fact, providing a rich culture of mentoring is precisely how average performers blossom into the high-performance category.

Over the past few years, I conducted an informal study on the culture of tennis facilities throughout my travels around the world. I came to some very predictable conclusions:

The programs with a positive culture were monitored and often reviewed by the owners. They were optimistic by design, and as a result, they achieved thriving, positive environments. They attracted top players organically via their triumphant athletes and their satisfied parents. They also acquired disgruntled clients from the negative cultured programs. As a result, the programs with a positive culture retained athletes up to three times as long as their problem-oriented rivals.

The programs with a problem-oriented drill Sargent culture struggled to keep coaches, to keep students, and to pay the rent. As a result, they had to partake in serious recruiting, sales, and marketing to just to keep their doors open.

CHAPTER 2: Sharpening Healthier Communication

It's dinner time at the Klein's house. Mr. Klein and his daughter Wendy spent the day at a USTA level 3 girls 16's event. Wendy was seeded #4 in the tournament. Her 9:00 am match went terribly wrong. Wendy's serve percentages were catastrophically low and as a result, she suffered an embarrassing first-round loss.

Later that night at the dinner table the conversation quickly escalated from small talk to another tennis-related screaming match. As they passed the potatoes, another family dinner was ruined. Mr. Klein wished he had an instruction manual for these heated exchanges.

Psychologists researching communication offer a concept called the Four-Sides Model. The theory states that Mr. Klein's initial comment "Honey, your serve was really off today." exposed four possible ways Wendy could accept the data:

1) As an impersonal factual stat.
2) Insights about Mr. Klein's feelings.
3) As a personal underlining insult towards Wendy.
4) As an appeal for improvement.

The message Mr. Klein was intentionally trying to convey isn't necessarily what was perceived by Wendy. Mr. Klein's statement "Honey, your serve was really off today." led to a whirlwind of problems between him and his daughter. This, in turn, spiraled into the silent treatment from his wife because once again their family harmony was disrupted.

For Mr. Klein, the factual data and appeal for improvement were the only reason for the statement. Wendy's interpretation of his statement was polar opposite. Wendy felt awful because she believed that she had let her parents and coaches down. She also concluded that her father's statement about her serve implied that she was not working hard enough and that she was a failure.

"Communication is less about what is being said and more about how the words are decoded by the listener."

As coaches and parents communicate with their athlete, the athlete's personality profile acts as a filter as they decode the information. Some athletes are wired to accept and enjoy the analysis of cold hard facts while others are wired to overlook the facts and instead zone into the emotional climate of the conversations. Each athlete connects the dots and paints the picture they choose to hear. An individual's personality profile determines how one communicates. (We will interpret personality profiles in greater detail in coming chapters.)

Is state of the art instruction about the instructor's proficiency in performing drills, or is it about the instructor's ability to connect with their student? Communicating above or below the digestion rate of the student is ineffective. While tennis knowledge and drilling efficiency are important, I believe a master teacher connects to the student and monitors the rate in which each student digests information. As we saw with Wendy and her father, the message received within the dialog is much more than the facts.

As I researched how to sharpen my communication skills, I realized that the way in which information is presented influences the outcome. I learned to focus on communicating honestly and with authenticity, but also to consider stressing or de-stressing the learning environment based on the energy in the room.

Successfully communicating the facts is highly dependent on WHAT message is being delivered and HOW the message is being delivered. The following list offers eight techniques I recommend applying to communicate effectively:

1) Intertwine sports science facts with personal, emotional storytelling.
2) Impart humor within a conversational tone to bond the relationship.
3) Avoid a distancing style with an elitist attitude and academic language.
4) Use inclusive pronouns like "We all need to…"
5) Apply cadences, rhythms, and dramatic pauses to accentuate meaning.
6) Vary their volume from a scream to a whisper to deepen the message.
7) Pull listeners in by modifying the pace of delivery from excited and fast to dramatic and slow.
8) Match and mirror the listener to make them more comfortable.

Great communicators presenting in groups or one-on-one have developed their presentation power. Armed with a full toolbox of delivery methods, they trade in intimidating, interrogating and dictating with sharing everyday experiences to engage the audience-which is the heart of genuinely connecting.

I Want To Be More Positive But What Do I Say?

Most parents and coaches want the very best for their children and students. However, finding the perfect words of comfort are not always easy, especially after competition. Regardless of the variations in personality profiles, parents and coaches alike need to reinforce the athlete's efforts with sincere non-judgmental encouraging words. The following is a list of insightful statements athletes need to hear after competition:

- I love watching you play!
- I'm so proud of you.
- I'm impressed by your skills.
- I'm so grateful to be your parent.
- You are so brave.
- It's so fascinating to watch you solve problems on court.
- You are so creative and skillful.
- I so admire your ability to stay focused on the court.
- It is so fun for me to watch you compete.
- I can't wait to hear what you think about the match.
- I admire your courage to compete.
- Your optimism is contagious- I love when you smile.
- This is my favorite part of the week.
- I love being your parent and/or coach.

Research shows that performing in the future as the Alpha competitor stems from a positive belief system. Your words become their inner dialogue. Emotional aptitude is a learned behavior. Your child's optimism and growth mindset should be molded daily. (Coach's Note: Please send the above insightful list to the parents of your athletes.)

All the great coaches I've met have a strong need for connecting and belonging. Positive communication is vital for a happy, longstanding career. Exceptional communication builds better relationships, mutual respect, and trust which leads to success. Superior coaching is the art of changing an athlete in a non-dictatorial way.

The student-coach connection improves with effective communication via verbal and nonverbal communication channels. The following chapters will uncover several excellent recommendations for coaches and parents to immerse themselves in the art of listening.

"When you talk, you are only repeating what you already know. But if you listen, you may learn something new."

Dalai Lama

CHAPTER 3: Effective Listening

The modern challenge of parenting and teaching tennis players is to let go of thinking like a repetitive "paint by the numbers" painter and to look at developing an athlete as a form of art. Teaching is art because each student is an original canvas.

Famous artists paint unique, one of a kind subjects and so should you. Don't be another painter, be an artist because teaching is art. If you're a "paint by the numbers" coach or parent, chances are you, and your athletes will never really be in high demand. Average parenting or coaching skills often produce average athletes. If you're a coach, think about the athlete's needs. Who wants to be an average athlete? No one! If you're a parent, your child doesn't need a well-intended yet mediocre tennis parent making the journey more difficult. They need a high IQ leader.

"We are taught how to read & write efficiently but not to speak and listen effectively."

The genesis of *The Soft Science of Tennis* for any parent or coach is to learn to be an effective listener. Effective listening is the ability to quietly give one's undivided attention which creates a more profound bond. Excellent communication between the athlete, coach, and parent is more than the typical dominating disciplinarian versus submissive student. Being listened to and understood is one of an athlete's greatest desires.

The method in which a parent or coach asks questions and listens is also important. If the athlete views the questions as an intimidating interrogation, they feel frightened and pressured. There is indeed an optimistic demeanor that encompasses effective listening.

Effective Listening Begins with:

- Get down, physically, to the students level.
- Take off your sunglasses and look them in the eyes.
- Give them your time. Listen intently.
- Assume you can learn from the student.
- Accept their view (set aside your beliefs).
- Allow them to lead, go with their flow.
- If you don't know the answer, say, "Let's explore that…"
- Understanding that talking "at" someone isn't power. Listening is power.
- Avoid speculating and jumping to conclusions.
- Maintain their conversational pace and fight the urge to interrupt.
- Allow them to finish their thoughts and sentences.
- Focus on spotting key objectives and phrases to discuss later.
- If you're planning witty responses, you're typically not actively listening.
- Remember, some athletes aren't seeking advice; they are seeking an empathetic ear.
- After discussing the issue, ask them for their solutions before offering your solutions.
- Ask them if they'd like to hear your thoughts.
- Avoid one-upmanship statements to prove that your past experience trumps theirs.
- Avoid saying, "I told you so!" Even when you told them so.

- Facilitate your relationship by applying empathy.
- Mirror their feelings within the context of their conversation.
- Follow their train of thought with nodding, caring facial expressions and body language.
- Re-state their points to clarify that you understand them correctly.
- Affirm their frustrations. "That sounds difficult, how did you respond?"
- To keep the focus on them, ask, "How did that make you feel? Versus "Here's what I would have done!"
- Conclude with a summarizing statement to ensure that their information was received correctly.
- Organize future, agreed upon solutions and job descriptions.

Those of us who fail to abide by the above guidelines send damaging subconscious "red flags" to the athlete in regards to the student-teacher relationship. Parents and coaches who are poor listeners send the following messages to their athletes:

- Your opinions and views aren't as important as mine.
- Your feelings are ridiculous and stupid.
- I'll explain your position more accurately than you.
- Listening to you is a waste of my precious time.
- I'm superior, stop talking and I'll prove it once again to you.
- There's nothing you can say that I haven't heard a million times.

Being a thoughtful teacher and communicator begins by being an empathetic listener. Great listeners change the student's perspective from a problem being a catastrophic event to an issue that is a solvable opportunity for growth.

Questions That Motivate Dialog

A great tool used to develop champions is to ask your athlete their opinion before you tell them your opinion. Questions can be based on an athlete's perception of their successes or failures.

Dialog producing examples include:

- "What was the cause of the winner or error?"
- "How did that feel when you?"
- "Were you paying attention to the opponent's?"
- "What was the highest percentage shot selection at that moment?"
- "If you could do it again, what would you do?"
- "What were you tactically trying to achieve?"
- "Are you staying on script?"

On and off the tennis court, winners are great problem solvers so avoid the parental and coaching temptation to solve all their problems for them. By doing so, you're robbing them of the exact skill sets needed to win tough future matches. In the big picture, listening to them versus talking "at" them is a much more enjoyable approach for the athlete. It sends the message of trust. It motivates them to take ownership of solution based thinking. With regards to keeping athletes in the game, customized student-based teaching is a fundamental missing link.

Verbal Communication in the Digital World

It's no secret that modern adolescents are obsessed with social media, tweeting, and texting. Kids are nurtured from the cradle to communicate through screens instead of interpersonal communication. They prefer texting over talking. It's the world in which they live.

Research in the field of communication found that a third of American teenagers send more than one-hundred texts a day. They want to feel a personal connection, engaged, inspired and understood…they just don't know how. The combination of their ineffective speaking skills combined with our weak listening skills is hurting the development process.

Listening "Between" the Words

Exceptional listeners filter through conversations to identify the true meaning behind their athlete's words. The ability to "listen" between words helps the listener discern if the student seeks constructive criticism or only a sympathetic ear. Attentive listeners recognize anomalies that enable them to identify the beliefs, attitudes, and feelings behind words. This allows them to interpret the athlete's spoken truth, fiction, optimism, pessimism, expectation, intentions, trust, past mental habits, and belief systems.

"An athlete's belief system crafts their future. Every syllable they speak engages energy towards them or against them."

As novice parents and intermediate coaches gain wisdom, they become more in-tune listeners. They discover hidden belief systems behind their athlete's dialog. Great listeners know there is "subconscious" energy behind words. Pessimistic behaviors are not difficult to spot because all too often, those very same negative thoughts, tones, words, and actions stem from those nurturing the athlete. As the athlete's thoughts become their words, those words determine their beliefs and play a deciding role in their performance, especially during stressful match conditions.

When effective listening is applied, the athlete's sequence of thought-speech-action becomes very clear to the "in-tuned" entourage. Please pay attention to the belief systems habitually used by your athletes. An athlete's affirmations and inner dialog can be categorized as optimistic or pessimistic. It should be painfully obvious that their self-coaching either builds them up or tears them down at crunch time.

Some athletes affirm positive results while others affirm catastrophe. Researchers continue to acknowledge the power thoughts have on one's actions. Studies show how thoughts, beliefs, and emotions affect human behavior. Following, I have listed a handful of tennis specific phrases from the mouths of our athletes and you can bet your life these habitual beliefs affect their match performance.

Pessimistic athletes project performance anxieties with statements such as:

- "I'm always worried about failing."
- "I'm not good enough for that level."
- "I'm not ready to compete."
- "I can't do it...I always blow it."
- "I'm not jealous but how is Kelly playing #1 and not me?"
- "I have to win tomorrow or my life is over."
- "I don't belong here."
- "I hate this...I hate that..."

Optimistic athletes project self-esteem and confidence with statements such as:

- "I can't wait to compete tomorrow."
- "I respect him but I'm going to beat him."
- "Competing is fun!"
- "I trained properly and I'm confident in my awesome ability."
- "I'm grateful for the privilege of playing."
- "I trust my game and problem-solving skills."
- "I love the competitive tennis lifestyle."
- "I appreciate all the love and support from my parents and coaches."

"A man is but the product of his thoughts - what he thinks, he becomes."

Mahatma Gandhi

Applying Positive Affirmations

If one's thoughts become one's reality, what exactly is a positive affirmation? A positive affirmation is a positive declaration or assertion. As optimistic thoughts sink into one's subconscious mind, they become a self-fulfilling prophecy over-riding old negative beliefs and habits with positive beliefs and rituals. Positive affirmations sound like silly fluff to specific personality profiles but they are proven methods of emotional improvement. When applied religiously, positive affirmations have the ability to rewire the chemistry in your athlete's brain. Elite athletes believe in their potential.

Assignment

Ask your athletes to customize ten positive affirmations that will help their self-esteem and confidence. Then ask them to read them aloud into their cell phone voice-recorder app. Finally, ask them to listen to their customized recording nightly as they are falling asleep. As they mentally rehearse their optimistic views, new solution based habits are formed and negative beliefs are dissolved.

Effective Listening doesn't stop with the verbal language. A great deal of information is available from the athlete without them saying a single word. The next chapter addresses the high IQ coach's secret ability to zero in on gathering critical information via non-verbal communication.

CHAPTER 4: Nonverbal Communication

Leading into our off-court, mental session Zoe asked "Please Coach Frank ... I just wanna hit! Can't Chloe and I just skip the mental stuff?" Most tennis parents would agree with their athletes. "Yeah, Frank...can't the girls get more grooving time in?" Not Mr. Potter. He's an ex-college standout and knows all too well the benefits of training the software components.

I asked the gals, "How is exclusively grooving those groundies working for ya?" "What do you mean?" asked Chloe? "Well, what's your UTR rating? I heard you both had trouble playing a pusher-retriever last week and profiling your opponents. Are you getting the results you're capable of achieving?" Suddenly the gals went silent. Mr. Potter added, "Zoe, the mental side of tennis is really important. We can stay longer and groove after Coach Frank addresses mental tennis. Would that be okay Frank?"

"Sure, I want to focus for 20 minutes on the importance of nonverbal communication in competition." The gals rolled their eyes as they dropped their racket bags and sat down in the club's classroom. I announced the day's topic as the girls looked to their phones… "Today's topic is the critical function of opponent profiling. Let's give this topic 20 minutes of focused attention and interaction and then we'll be done for the day. Anyone that wants to groove more groundstrokes can stay longer. Deal? I'll start with a few open-ended questions."

- *Why is it important to identify the opponent's style of play?*
- *What are the benefits of spotting stroke & movement strengths & weaknesses?*
- *Would it be meaningful to decipher the opponent's most proficient patterns of play?*
- *How would knowing their shot tolerance help you strategize?*
- *Would knowing what frustrates them help in match play?*

The gals initially were stumped, but after a brief discussion, hit the bull's eye with their answers. I asked them one last question, "Why does opponent profiling fall into the category of nonverbal communication?"

"Girls... I got this one!" Mr. Potter added from the back of the room. "The opponent isn't going to tell you their weaknesses. In matches, you've got to develop the skill of reading the opponent. Am I right or am I right!"

At first, profiling athletes through their nonverbal communication seems like reading the invisible but trust me, after a bit of training it becomes as reliable as feeding another basket of tennis balls. Our conscious minds pay attention to the verbal message, the message within the dialog. Our subconscious minds pay attention to nonverbal clues such as tone of voice and body language.

Over the years of focusing on the most effective coaching methods, the importance of nonverbal communication became very clear. I found that an athlete's words were often only part of their story. Communication research has found that a subject's actual words to be the least revealing of their true feelings or comfort level, giving more importance to a subject's tone of voice, facial expression and body language. It is critical that the coach be able to recognize the athlete's nonverbal cues because it enhances the learning experience and enables the coach to better understand how the athlete is wired. It is also important to note the athlete's parent's nonverbal cues because the parents play a vital role in their child's success. Let's dive into a handful of these critical non-verbal clues to help you begin to profile your athletes.

Appearance

When coaching, I make it a point to notice my athlete's appearance, clothing choice, and organization of equipment. Is Sarah's hair braided to perfection? Does her Nike skirt match perfectly with her Nike top, Nike socks, Nike shoes, and Nike warm-ups? This indicates to me an SJ (Sensing, Judging) persona.

Do Sam's Wilson Blade rackets have different gauge strings, different brand dampeners with non-matching over-grips? Does he carry them in a Head racket bag with a Prince water bottle? This initially indicates to me an NP (Intuitive, Perceiver) personality. I realize that exceptions shadow every rule, so these initial non-verbal clues are observational hunches that begin to shed light on their personality profile.

Posture

I then assess the athlete's body posture throughout our session, both during off-court conversations and on-court performance, which helps me to determine their self-esteem and confidence levels. Defensive attitudes are often shown by crossed arms and slumped shoulders. Students lean-in or walk towards the net when they're interested. In my opinion, confidence or lack thereof is also identified by the athlete's swagger or timid posture and stance.

Eyes

Throughout my coaching sessions, I also pay close attention to the athlete's eyes. The old saying is "The eyes are the gateway to the soul." Spotting if a student is dialed in and focused on the task at hand or mentally gone can be detected in their eyes. Are they telling the truth or fibbing? Athletes' emotional state such as being upset, tranquil, content or angry can also be detected in their eyes.

Facial Expressions

Interpreting an athlete's facial expression can also help a coach profile their athletes. Obviously, students show emotion through their facial expressions. Squinting eyes and tight lips are signs of anger, tension, and frustration. Smiles are signs of comfort and confidence. I can often tell if an athlete or parent isn't buying the information I'm providing by interpreting their facial expressions.

Tone of Voice

Observing their tone of voice is another essential clue I use to profile athletes. The tone of voice doesn't communicate logic, but it does convey the athlete's feelings.

"An athlete's tone of voice speaks the truth even when their words don't."

Effective Communication is dependent on tone. The same word said with a different tone can often imply the opposite meaning to the listener. I find this true when assisting parents and their athletes. The parent's words frequently say one thing and their tone says the polar opposite. Athletes listen to their parent's tone and tune out their parent's words because their tone reflects their true feelings, tension and attitude.

Throughout your sessions, pay attention as the athletes expose flashes of their inborn personality. An introvert's theoretic response, an intuitive gut-action, a feelers empathetic reaction or a perceiver's future speculation speaks volumes. Once dialed into the inner world of your athlete's brain designs you'll be able to connect with each athlete's overall persona and customize your training to their unique needs. As high-performance tennis coaches or parents, it's our job to get into each student's world, instead of demanding that they get into ours.

Utilizing Written Communication

The human brain is divided into several regions. Each region processes different forms of incoming information. Listening to verbal instruction engages the auditory region of the brain, while physically writing notes engages the spatial awareness region of the brain. Athletes who collect data in two regions of the brain have a greater chance of retaining a higher proportion of key facts and recalling the information later in competition.

Post Lesson Written Reviews

I have been applying post lesson written reviews for decades. My athletes are encouraged to take the last few minutes of their training session to write down their top lesson topics and future action plans. Some of my current students still prefer the old school paper and pen journaling while others use their cell phone notepad and to-do apps. Either way, written reminders are an important version of nonverbal communication.

Benefits Include:

- Writing lesson reviews work to preview the athlete's developmental plan via time management.
- Documenting helps to de-stress and relax the athlete as it unloads cognitive baggage. Athletes can read and re-read their notes to review the lesson.
- It's estimated that within 24 hours, up to 80% of what our students learn they soon forget. Writing it down helps athletes to digest more information.
- Writing down important solutions helps re-enforce recall. It enables the athlete to memorize more efficiently and recall as needed.
- Documenting assists in organizing and assimilating the new information received.
- Writing down solutions act as the first visualization rehearsal further solidifying the memorization of the data.

The Soft Science of Tennis aims to improve the learning curve. Applying these methods maximize athletic potential at a quicker rate.

CHAPTER 5: Personality Based Training

"Personality profiling assists coaches, athletes, and parents in understanding how individuals gather information and make decisions. It's how we are wired. It's what makes us tick."

Personality Based Training (PBT) is a training method that focuses the attention on the athlete's unique brain design as opposed to the educator. When applying PBT, tennis pros and parents welcome and respect the athlete's unique preferred styles of learning, behaving and playing the game. The athletes feel empowered because their views and needs are recognized. And once understood, students are more motivated and inspired to learn and improve. An inspired student is more likely to take the leadership role in achieving their goals.

"Athletes would benefit from understanding the advantages and disadvantages of their unique brain design. It's why they are naturally good at some things and uncomfortable with others."

It's important to note that while I've studied sports psychology for the past 30 years, I am a veteran, "In the Trenches" practical application tennis coach, not an "Academia" psychologist. But neither were Katharine Briggs and her daughter Isabel Myers, authors of the famous Myers-Briggs Type Indicator (MBTI- A psychological questionnaire used to understand individuals mental preferences.) published in the United States in 1943. Together Myers-Briggs noticed that individuals have different temperaments and unique ways of seeing the world.

While some scientists say the MBTI doesn't stand up to scientific reliability, I can say with all honesty that it has helped me coach over 100 National Champions and several Pro tour athletes. More importantly, personality profiling benefits my athletes and their entourage of parents, coaches, and trainers at a much deeper level. A study conducted by Psychology Today, reports that approximately 80% of Fortune 500 companies use various personality tests to hire future employees, to assess progress, and to maximize efficiency and harmony through team building events. The time has come to broaden the role of personality profiling into the athletic realm, as I have outlined in *The Soft Science of Tennis*.

Getting to know the Myers-Briggs Type Indicator (MBTI)

The MBTI is the most popular psychometric questionnaire designed to measure psychological preferences in how people perceive the world and make decisions. It's my intention to bring to light the usefulness of brain preference identification in the tennis industry. Each student has a preferred way of seeing the world. The basic MBTI theory categorizes preferences into four groups from which individuals identify their dominant cerebral preference.

The Typographies Include:

- **Extraversion** ("E")- People/Places
- **Introversion** ("I")- Theories/ Information

- **Sensing** ("S")- Facts/Reality
- **Intuition** ("N") Possibilities/Potential

- **Thinking** ("T")- Logic/Truthfulness
- **Feeling** ("F")- Harmony/Relationships

- **Judgment** ("J")- Orderly/Structured
- **Perception** ("P")- Flexible/Adaptable

For each of the above pairings, your athletes typically have a preference for one system above the other. The combination of their four preferences gives them their initial assessment in a four-letter acronym. An example is personality profile: ISTP (Introvert Sensate Thinker Perceiver)

"View your athlete's brain design (dominant and auxiliary) the same way you would view right handed versus left handed body type functions.
Each athlete has an inborn preferred system."

In my experience, personality profiling is a soft science, meaning other factors such as nurturing and environments skew the data. With that said, I believe that athletes have specific preferences in the way they experience the world and these choices affect their actions, values, and motivational needs on and off the tennis court.

Universal Truths

- Gaining an understanding of this soft science takes time. Be patient as you learn to apply this new found skill. I encourage you to apply personality profiling as a means to understand how students tick versus stereotyping or grouping athletes by mere age or general ability.

- Coaches can't change an athlete's primary brain design, but they can nurture both the individual's weaker, opposing profile and strengthen their dominant profile.

- Interestingly, on rare occasions, a student's on-court persona opposes their off-court persona.

- Everyone exhibits both dominant and auxiliary traits. For example, introverts can be quite sociable for short stints of time.

- There isn't a right, wrong, superior, or inferior type, but rather preferred approaches to the game and life. Although there are only 16 unique brain design categories, everyone is unique. For example, there is a broad spectrum of each preference ranging from moderate to extreme.

- All brain designs need to devote time and energy to nurturing their non-dominant functions.

- It is not unlikely for athletes young and old to inaccurately self-profile their brain design to fit into a more popular, cool version of themselves.

- Pay attention to other's brain design because this is why opposite types make you crazy and similar types make you comfortable.

- An athlete will benefit significantly from understanding the advantages and disadvantages of their unique design.

- Customized development through personality profiling increases self-esteem and breeds confidence, which is seen in the athlete's peaceful performance.

- Profiling your athlete's personalities won't provide you with the final answers, but it will assist in organizing their unique developmental pathways, which will maximize enjoyment, as well as help them to reach their potential at a quicker rate.

- It's our job as educators and parents to de-code each athlete, so we are better equipped to assist them in maximizing their potential.

- Due to the combination of nature and nurture, exceptions shadow every rule in the soft science of personality profiling.

In chapters 8-11, challenges and dominant solutions are presented to help understand the specific cerebral designs. It is important to note that many of the given solutions may also be used with other cognitive types.

The following chapters uncover the valuable benefits that result from revealing the mental typographies of our athletes.

CHAPTER 6: Benefits of Personality Profiling

Caroline Sanchez was a top 50 ITF junior in her day. She played D-2 college ball in Florida and competed on the challenger circuit for three years earning her a world ranking of #676 on the WTA Tour. Caroline sounds like an experienced competitor, but is she the right fit for your player's coaching needs?

Let's take a more in-depth look at Caroline's background. Caroline grew up on the slow red clay in Barcelona where her coaches demanded she train and play the "Spanish Way" - steady, retriever style. Caroline possesses solid groundstrokes, great lateral movement, and a 20 ball shot tolerance level. She loves to camp 15 feet behind the baseline and extend points in a retriever fashion. Like her past coaches, she's been nurtured to be an old-school drill sergeant style of coach and demands every student train and play in the style that she found to be most successful.

Coaches, is she a good fit for your program? Parents, is she a good fit for your child? The answer: No, not likely, unless all your athletes are wired with the same exact cognitive brain design, body type, and temperament which would be extremely rare. Coaches who only teach the system that they found to be successful regardless of the student's needs are doing a disservice to the athlete. Tennis playing styles are an extension of the athlete's brain design and body type. An athlete's most successful style of play incorporates their inherent strengths versus their coach's past strengths.

Devising an athlete's developmental plan is the ideal time to incorporate their personality profile. Training and nurturing athletes to play the style that flows with their genetic predispositions and not against it will maximize their potential at a much faster rate.

As I travel around the globe, I notice that coaches and parents religiously focus on the development of the athlete's hardware (strokes and athleticism) yet tend to neglect the critical development of their student's software (mental and emotional). Personality profiling falls into the software or soft science of teaching tennis.

"Coaches and parents who understand the athlete's personality in greater depth utilize a more comprehensive foundation from which to maximize performance."

A simple analogy is a comparison between the four main tennis components (strokes, athleticism, mental and emotional) with a conventional four-legged table. A table with four-legs is not stable under stress without all four legs intact. The same holds true for your tennis athletes.

So, how does the understanding of the software development relate to you as parents, coaches, tennis directors or club managers? It develops a greater understanding of how others tick and that sets you and your players above the competition. Software assessment helps us to understand how individuals perform as tennis players. It assists coaches and parents in developing much more than strokes. It helps shape positive character traits, life skills, and a moral compass.

The Benefits of Personality Profiling Include:

- ☐ Customizing the Athlete's Developmental Plan
- ☐ Assessing Mental Strengths and Weaknesses
- ☐ Assessing Emotional Efficiencies and Deficiencies
- ☐ Identifying Information Processing / Listening Skills
- ☐ Facilitating Conflict Avoidance and Resolution
- ☐ Empowering Communication Strategies
- ☐ Encouraging the Development of Synergy and Harmony within their Entourage
- ☐ Monitoring Self-Awareness and the Awareness of Other Personality Profiles
- ☐ Acknowledging and Respecting Differing Brain Designs
- ☐ Identifying Productive Communication Avenues
- ☐ Assisting in Identifying Motivational Factors
- ☐ Improving Productivity and Efficiency

Benefits to Athletes:

In the soft science realms of confidence, trust, and self-esteem, there's power to be gained from athletes celebrating their profile. Gaining the knowledge of how they see the world makes the soft science of personality profiling helpful in working with varying styles of coaches and teachers. The quicker those athletes understand their cognitive design the more successful they will be at understanding their style of play and customizing their developmental pathway.

The following chapter gets into the nitty-gritty of how your athlete's cognitive design affects their performance. Hold on tight because I'm about to blow your mind as I uncover commonalities of each typography.

CHAPTER 7: How the Brain Affects Performance

"Athletes who share similar cerebral inner workings also share mental and emotional strengths and weaknesses in the competitive arena."

This chapter will uncover how brain design affects tennis performances. The following brain design categories can be used as an informal observation as you first profile yourself. However, I suggest going online to the dozens of more in-depth questionnaires. Choose the accuracy and depth of the personality profiling questionnaire that is right for you. After a bit of research, you will recognize learning preferences that best describe your brain design.

Let's review the basics from earlier in this book. There are 16 configurations of personality profiles found around the world. By completing your chosen questionnaire, you will discover your association – a 4-letter acronym nicknaming your personality profile. Once comfortable with the terminology, you will be able to categorize your athletes into their unique design. Following is a list of commonalities I've uncovered on-court with my high-performance students.

Uncovering Your Students Typography

Introverts (I) versus Extroverts (E)

Introvert Students

- Reserved, reflective thinkers.
- Prefer concrete advice versus abstract thinking.
- Need quiet, alone time to recharge their batteries.
- Prefer to blend into groups versus stand out.
- Energy conserving, private and quiet individuals.
- Enjoy the one-on-one settings of private lessons over group lessons.
- Prefer to retaliate in match play versus instigate action.

Extrovert Students

- Enjoy the energy in group lessons with lots of people.
- Enjoy the limelight, center court, and center stage.
- Vocally and physically expressive on court.
- Easily bored with mundane repetition.
- Prefer to make things happen in matches versus retrieving.
- View tournaments as social environments.
- Work best in short attention span type drills.
- Strangers are friends they haven't met yet.
- Benefit from stretches of silent tennis drilling.

"Coaching confusion takes place when an athlete's body type (size, speed, agility, strength) opposes their hidden inner workings.

For example, the athlete body type appears to be designed to instigate action by capturing the net, but they religiously choose to stay back and retaliate instead. Typically brain design over-rides body design."

Sensate (S) versus Intuitive (N)

Sensate Students

- Choose to make decisions after analyzing.
- Often hesitate on-court due to over thinking.
- Thrive on the coaches facts versus opinions.
- Enjoy practical details versus the "Do it cuz I said so!" method.
- Need to know when and why not just how.
- Success on-court is based on personal experience not theory.
- Pragmatic need for sports science rational.
- Comfortable backcourt players where they have more decision-making time.
- Prefer organized, structured lessons versus time-wasting ad-lib sessions.

Intuitive Students

- Trust their gut instinct and hunches over detailed facts.
- In matches, often do first then analyze second.
- Apply and trust their imagination with creative shot selection.
- Thrive on new, exciting opportunities on the practice court.
- In discussions are less interested in minute details and facts.
- Learn quicker by being shown versus lengthy verbal explanations of the drill.
- Seek the creative approach to the game.
- Natural born offensive net rushers and poachers in doubles.
- Enjoy coaches' metaphors and analogies.

- Often have to be reminded of the reality of the situation.

"PET scan and sensing perception studies from the University of Iowa show that different brain designs use various parts of their brain. Athletes are pre-wired with their genetics. Teaching them to compete on-court within their natural guidelines versus opposing those guidelines will maximize their potential and enjoyment of our great sport.

An analogy to illustrate this point is swimming downstream and working within one's genetic predisposition versus swimming upstream and working against one's genetic predisposition. While it is possible to find success outside one's dominant brain design, it is much more difficult."

Thinkers (T) versus Feelers (F)

Thinker Students

- Impersonalize tennis matches in a business fashion.
- Continually analyze the pros and cons of each situation.
- Thrive in private lessons versus group activities.
- In discussions, they are frank and often void of tactfulness.
- Aware of coaching inconsistencies.
- In competition, they are less influenced by emotions than other brain designs.
- Prefer logical explanations versus hunches.
- Relate to technical skills training over mental or emotional skills training.
- Less concerned about personal interaction and group harmony.
- Prefer work before play even in practice.
- Value fairness and good sportsmanship.
- Often seen as uncaring or indifferent to others.

Feeler Students

- Enjoy group sessions with their peers.
- Often put others needs ahead of their needs.
- Strong need for optimism and harmony on-court.
- Struggle with match play cheating and gamesmanship.
- Usually outcome-oriented versus process-oriented.
- Perform with their heart versus their head.
- Often miss the details and facts in problem-solving.
- Sometimes too empathetic to struggling opponents.
- Need frequent process reminders to regain focus.

"A gender stereotype myth is that females are feelers and males are thinkers. While the exact percentages vary widely from study to study, it's clear that brain function doesn't necessarily correlate with gender. Nature versus nurture falls into play.

Though societal bias may nurture females to be more nurturing and caring and males to be more tough problem-solvers, females can be genetically wired to be thinkers just as males can be wired to be feelers."

Judgers (J) versus Perceivers (P)

Judger Students

- Prefer planned, orderly structured lessons.
- Often postpone competing because they're not 100% ready.
- Are frequently afraid to make the wrong decision, so they freeze up in competition.
- Need closure with a task before moving onto the next drill.
- Enjoy making detailed lists to ensure productivity.
- Have a strong need to control most aspects of situations.
- Change is uncomfortable and is typically shunned.
- Multitasking is avoided, as they prefer to focus on one component at a time.
- Rules and laws apply to them and everyone else in the academy.
- Often closed-minded to new information until its proven correct.
- Often more-fixed-mind-set versus growth-mind-set.
- Self-regulated and enjoy working their customized developmental plan.

Perceiver Students

- In competition, perceivers are mentally found in the future, not the present.
- Often struggle with closing out leads in matches.
- Day-dream and often struggle with remaining on task.
- Are flexible and spontaneous.
- Easily adapt to the ever-changing match situations.
- Open to discussing and applying new, unproven concepts.

- Often more growth-mind-set versus fixed-mindset.
- Appear relaxed and loose under stress.
- Perform in cycles of energy.
- Typically need goal dates and deadlines to work hard.
- In matches, focus on outcome scenarios versus performance play.
- Often postpone training until the last minute.

"Athletes who make the most significant gains are independent thinkers who are self-aware of their inborn characteristics, strengths, and weaknesses. Understanding your player's personality profile will enrich your relationships and assist you in helping your students develop excellent technique, athleticism, strategies and handling stress under pressure."

Take a few moments, sit back and digest the above information. I'm sure you will smile as you systematically place specific students, co-workers, friends and family members into their genetic predispositions.

In chapters 8- 11, four customized challenges and their solutions are provided for each of the sixteen personality profiles.

CHAPTER 8: Assisting the 4 SP Typographies

ESTP, ISTP, ISFP, ESFP

ESTP- Extrovert Sensate Thinker Perceiver

Challenge: ESTP's are natural born entertainers and love to play on center court. To their detriment, they often choose to play to the spectators applying crowd-pleasing, low percentage, shot selections.

Solution: It's important to allow ESTP's the freedom to express themselves while keeping them in the match play modes of proper offense, neutral and defensive shot options. A critical game plan for thrill-seeking ESTP's is only to hit the shot the moment demands.

Challenge: Focusing on the moment at hand is a task ESTP's often struggle to sustain. These adaptable, outgoing individuals are usually physically gifted but are impulsive and get distracted from routinely sticking to high percentage plays.

Solution: Teach them to design and rehearse their script of customized percentage patterns of play. Educate them on the fact that if those patterns are winning 2 out of 3 points, there's no need to interject change. Victories will pile up if you can get ESTP's to hit the same old boring winners set after set.

Challenge: ESTP's are not designed to stand in line and conform to the masses. They do not see the value in rigidly enforced nonessential rules. Lighten your sessions with laughter. This brain design doesn't work well with excessively inflexible mentors. Due to their EP design, you can spot these unique individuals because they often choose flashy attire and beat to their drum.

Solution: Forget about extinguishing their unique flame. Focus on soft guidance versus ridged control. ESTP's are flashy players who enjoy going for bold winners. Forcing them to stand 15 feet behind the baseline and grind week in-week out doesn't fit their genetic design.

Challenge: ESTP's often apply unnecessary risk in competition. They typically get bored without a challenge and occasionally go "off the boil" as our friends down under like to say.

Solution: Ask these athletes to apply a personal challenge when boredom creeps in. The mission is for the student to focus on routinely winning 3 points in a row. This mental drill forces them to eliminate their wandering mind as they zero in to win. Remind them of the WIN acronym: What's Important Now!

ISTP- Introvert Sensate Thinker Perceivers

Challenge: ISTP's are bold, courageous competitors-fighting until the bitter end. Often young ISTP's believe they have little use for boring fundamentals. "Open the can... serve'em up" is their battle cry.

Solution: Make fundamental stroke building into a competitive game, not a chore. Mundane, repetitive drills bore them to tears. Add negative scoring to each basic drill to keep the competitor interested. Rallying for hours on end is a surefire way to lose this great athlete to another sport.

Challenge: On the stress-free practice court, ISTP's will digest detail. They're not content with simple instructions on how to hit a ball; ISTP's want to know where, when, and why. But, in live-ball sparing scenarios, this type dials in their competitive focus and doesn't want a ton of instruction.

Solution: In private tennis lessons, explain who, what, where, why, when. This information ties into their sensing typography. In live ball sessions, allow them time to process themselves. Instead of talking, shadow swing the stroke or pattern so they can visualize and perceive the proper sequence.

Challenge: ISTP's aren't initially comfortable with coaches or teammates with opposing brain designs. Due to their thinking design, they can be sensitive to their feelings yet cold and impersonal when it comes to the feelings of others. Accepting other's points of view can be difficult.

Solution: Educate emotional intelligence along with logic. Remind ISTP's that their cerebral design is merely one of the 16 different personality profile categories and each profile has varying preferred learning processes. Reinforce the fact that everyone is not wired like them and it is possible they aren't always right.

Challenge: The ISTP's distinctive patterns of thinking, feeling and behaving have made them favorites in the field of sports psychology type based assessments. While high-performance ISTP athletes prosper in the hardware department, they often languish in the development of their software.

Solution: Early in their development, put forth great effort into building their life skills, especially relationship skills. ISTP's often struggle with finding the right words to nurture their alliances optimistically. Out-going people often aggravate strong ISTP's. They may find an extroverted, feeler coach or teammate suffocating so they prefer to reject the much-needed affiliation.

ISFP: Introvert Sensate Feeler Perceiver

Challenge: ISFP athletes tend to have their own agendas and schedules. They "beat to their own drum." The structure and rules of others are often difficult for them to follow.

Solution: When too many demands and obligations fall upon them, these introverted individuals need alone time to recharge their batteries. Their SF function makes them want to do everything correctly to make others proud. Provide information and instruction at a rate that is comfortable for them to digest so that they can better assimilate. Excessive details tend to bog down ISFP's.

Challenge: Pay particular attention to the amount of criticism offered to the ISFP. Lack of appreciation is a sure fire way for them to pull away from the sport.

Solution: Apply the five-compliments to one-criticism approach when working with this cerebral design. Use video analysis to point out their incredible strengths and improvements instead of only their weaknesses and failures. Instead of offering advice in the heat of the moment, offer to be available to chat when they're ready to talk through their feelings.

Challenge: Under stress, this type can become excessively critical of themselves and others trying to assist them. These athletes tend to be harsh as they obsess over their mistakes and imagined problems.

Solution: Validate that you understand their feelings but reassure them that feelings are simply emotions and emotions are often speculations, not absolute facts. Have some fun as you remind them that their catastrophic thoughts are just thoughts and often not reality.

Challenge: Due to their FP design, these individuals are likely to mentally drift into future thoughts after a lead is established. These outcome thoughts include: "what's my ranking going to be?", "Who do I play next?", "What are my friends going to say when I beat this top seed?".

Solution: Assist the ISFP's in remaining on script, within their performance state of mind after they've built a lead. Drifting into outcome-oriented scenarios while still in the match is a receipt for disaster.

ESFP: Extrovert Sensate Feeler Perceiver

Challenge: ESFP's are performers at heart. They'd often prefer to daydream about the big moment versus relentlessly preparing for it.

Solution: Accountability is vital. Assist them in customizing their detailed developmental blueprint within their weekly planners. They're more likely to accept the rules if they view the rules as their rules instead of a parent or coaches demands.

Challenge: ESFP athletes typically learn best by doing (kinesthetic) versus listening (Auditory). Sitting still and listening to a coach or parent's theories for extended periods is a waste of time for this type.

Solution: Offer short 1- minute sound bites and snippets of pertinent information throughout their hitting sessions. The kiss of death for this cerebral design is the coach that talks at the student for 45- minutes of their 1- hour lesson.

Challenge: ESFP's are optimistic, friendly athletes but can turn negative in a passive resistant manner when they begin to feel unstimulated, especially in group lessons.

Solution: Look for nonverbal clues such as their wandering eyes and mind. Detecting that you have lost their attention is the first step in regaining their attention. Add customized, personal challenges to these types to keep them zeroed into the task at hand.

Challenge: EF's are often easy marks for opponent's who apply gamesmanship. Their genetic need for peace and harmony can complicate the drama found as the opponent employs their "creative line calls."

Solution: Preset step by step solutions to handling gamesmanship. Discuss why cheaters cheat and why it's often a successful tactic at the beginner and intermediate levels but not as athletes mature and soft skill sets are developed- such as perseverance, resiliency or conquering performance anxieties. Explain the neuroscience of channel capacity. (The human brain cannot solve two complicated tasks simultaneously). By pulling the ESFP into the drama "channel," this type unknowingly aborts the all-important performance goals "channel." The result is a significant drop in performance level.

CHAPTER 9: Assisting the 4 NF Typographies
INFP, ENFP, INFJ, ENFJ

INFP: Introvert Intuitive Feeler Perceiver

Challenge: INFP's aren't wired to enjoy analyzing match data. Their P brain design makes them "big picture" athletes versus "students of the game" who enjoy number crunching and quantifying data.

Solution: Trade in detailed date match charts like the typical errors to winners chart and replace it with a court positioning chart. The court positioning chart provides the big picture INFP's can sink their teeth into and understand. Chart points won/lost when playing behind the court versus points won/lost when played inside the court.

Challenge: INFP's are athletes who are often a bit overly sensitive to criticism. Detailed lists of "Here's what you're doing wrong..." stress out this profile more than most.

Solution: Apply authenticity while offering up their strengths versus weaknesses. They see tennis as an expressive game. If they feel their creativity stifled, they shut down, and effort is lost. Feelers are sensitive. Apply extra doses of optimism to their training regimen.

Challenge: This rare brain design is warm and kind but at the same time challenging to satisfy. After matches, they are typically their own toughest critics. These students try desperately to please friends, teammates, parents, and coaches which often leaves them drained.

Solution: Motivate the INFP to shoot for daily excellence in their training and match play versus perfection. Athletes in need of perfection in order to be happy suffer foolishly. Assist them in organizing their weekly developmental plan and making themselves the priority during those times.

Challenge: These friendly, quiet introverts don't have the natural spatial design to take in large doses of auditory information. Like a few other cerebral designs, talking at them isn't in the parent, coach, or student's best interest.

Solution: Getting into their work requires identifying their preferred learning system. INFP's are visual learners that prefer to imitate a coach's actions. When working with this type, demonstrate the skill you are seeking, and they will effortlessly copy the movements. Encourage them to attend college or professional tennis matches and visualize themselves performing in that environment.

ENFP: Extrovert Intuitive Feeler Perceiver

Challenge: ENFP's are creative, outside the box thinkers. For them, stepping outside of their comfort zone is easy. Instead of rigidly adhering to mundane rules and regulations, ENFP's simply work around them.

Solution: Avoid micromanaging this type. A trick to coaching the ENFP is to keep drills fresh. Rallying to 100 is not only non-practical but will bore them to tears. Instead, customize 2-3 ball patterns based on the athlete's offense, neutral and defensive situations. Challenge them to stay focused until they complete the exercise 10 times. Add negative scoring (deduct one from their score for each error) to improve their focus ability and their emotional component along with their hardware.

Challenge: The downfall of being extroverted is that ENFP's are often in high demand. They repeatedly have trouble saying no when friends, family, acquaintances or even strangers ask for their help. Their empathetic nature is their blessing and their curse. This occasionally overwhelms the EF type, and they need to shut down and IT (Introvert/Think) for a bit.

Solution: Coaches should be on the lookout for signs of extrovert burn out. Symptoms include a noticeable shift in character. Such as when their natural optimism is turning pessimistic or when this popular, friendly type begins to act less approachable, sharp-tongued and uncaring. At this time, motivate them to take some time off to recharge their batteries.

Challenge: ENFP's are social and energetic tennis players. Their EF traits make them infectious partners and tennis teammates. They are natural investigators and explorers who get quickly bored with routine. Multitasking, communication, and people skills are their strong suit, but their problem solving and focus skills on-court may need your attention.

Solution: ENFP's are future-minded, big picture athletes. On-court they can struggle with keeping their mind focused "In the game." Disinterested with the past and even the present, these types have to be reminded to stay focused on this stroke, this tactical play, and only this point. Coaches would be wise to develop their match closure skills.

Challenge: ENFP's prefer to rely on their intuition and flow subconsciously through competition. Coaches can spot the moment when these NFP types stop playing in-the-moment and begin to think about the outcome. Examples include: "Man, I'm up 4-1 versus the top seed. I can win this…then boom!" They just traded in their intuitive, performance state of mind for a sensate overwhelming outcome mindset. Or "I'm down 2-5, I'm gonna lose anyway so I might as well relax and go for my shots…Boom!" They win three straight games to 5-5 only to flip the switch back to over-thinking about the outcome and drop the set 5-7.

Solution: Designing their strategic script of customized top patterns and ingrain them through pattern repetition, dress rehearsal, and practice match play. Teaching an ENFP to close out points, games, sets, and matches while staying on script is the key to developing their competitive focus.

INFJ: Introvert Intuitive Feeler Judger

Challenge: Unfamiliarity is a sensitive topic for the INFJ's. Adaptability isn't their strong suit.

Solution: Entering competition, arrive at the new tournament site early to hit. Allow this athlete a bit more time to get comfortable with the elements, the court speed, club, and other environmental differences. Also, scouting of future opponents is comforting to this cerebral design. While profiling the next opponent, it is wise to discuss their style of play, their "go-to patterns," their stroke and movement efficiencies and deficiencies and their shot tolerance.

Challenge: INFJ's prefer quiet, calm training environments with little interruptions. Too much socialization in group scenarios is distracting and illogical to this IJ typography.

Solution: If they believe that the practice environment is unproductive, they begin to feel fragmented and disconnected to their developmental plan. Coaches would be wise to begin sessions with a short preview of the day's focal points, analyses, and evaluate throughout the session. And then later review with the athletes their thoughts in regards to their success rate accomplishing their daily goals.

Challenge: INFJ's have vivid imaginations, which they use to, pre-set their ideal perfect conditions and solutions. Lawyers call this "speculation." When reality doesn't conform to their pre-set version, their imagined perfection is lost, and their will to fight is shattered.

Solution: Ask them a philosophical question: "Is this world perfect? Their obvious answer is no." Then offer: "If God couldn't make a perfect world ...why do you think you should be perfect?" The competitive game of tennis is messy and imperfect. It's best to encourage your athletes to shoot for near excellent performances on a consistent basis instead of perfection and let go of their pre-match speculations.

Challenge: INFJ tennis players are feelers who can be overly sensitive to criticism. When coaches challenge their logical decision making, they're likely to get an aggressive comeback. Rigid IJ's actively dislike being proven wrong. After a high percentage shot selection tip from the coach, they'll likely seek the exception to the rule and throw out a "Yeah but ..." response.

Solution: Explain winning percentages on the tennis court is merely 2 out of 3. Winning 66% of the points is excellent. No one should be expected to win 100% of the points in any given situation. Also, teaching pros should gently remind athletes that exceptions follow every rule in life. In high-percentage tennis, seek to follow the rules approximately eighty percent of the time, while seeking the exception to the rule approximately twenty percent of the time.

ENFJ: Extrovert Intuitive Feeler Judger

Challenge: ENFJ's are often a bit naive and idealistic. They struggle when the competition gets tense, and confrontation arises. This brain design enjoys the socialization and athleticism of the game but gets disillusioned when unnecessary emotional drama comes into play. They can shut down and disassociate themselves under pressure.

Solution: Since confrontation is at the heart of competition, it's wise to educate the ENFJ students to get comfortable in uncomfortable situations. Role play formulas to assist your athletes in making peace with nurturing the alpha competitor inside. Practice sessions should include rehearsing protocols against opponents who hook, flip the score, stall or intimidate these athletes.

Challenge: Due to their EF traits, ENFJ brain designs are emotional competitors. On the upside, these charismatic leaders are typically witnessed cheering for their friends and teammates. However, in their own competition, ENFJ's can quickly turn negative.

Solution: This design also needs more than their fair share of encouragement. Coaches in tune with the emotional components of athletes should realize that this squeaky wheel NEEDS the grease. Meaning, it's often the givers who need the parents and teaching pro's approval, praise and positive affirmations just as much as the more demanding, pessimistic students.

Challenge: When coaching FJ's, it's important to note that they're often highly sensitive to disapproval. Being proven wrong in their decisions doesn't sit lightly for J types.

Solution: To maintain their high level of self-esteem, a trick of the trade is to use reverse psychology in your teaching. For example, if the ENFJ's still tossing the ball too high on their serve, replace "Geez Joey, I've told you 100 times... toss slightly above the peak of your reach!" with "Nice Joey! You're starting to get the apex of the toss right above your strike zone. You must have lowered your toss 3 feet!" Of course, Joey didn't lower his toss yet but guess who's more likely to improve his toss and whose ego won't plummet by being proven wrong?

Challenge: While this J type is usually keenly organized, under match day stress, they perform primarily within their NF functions. I've witnessed countless times that ENFJ's play from the gut. NF's who abort their preset script of proactive patterns and choose to go off script usually end up making reckless shot selections.

Solution: Educate the athlete to understand that winning stems from practicing in the manner in which they are expected to perform and then to perform in the manner in which they have been practicing. Remaining on script is critical because it provides them with opportunities to do what they do best at crunch time.

CHAPTER 10: Assisting the 4 NT Typographies
ENTJ, INTP, ENTP, INTJ

ENTJ: Extrovert Intuitive Thinker Judger

Challenge: "Give me the facts and let's get to work" is this athlete's motto. TJ's have little use for small talk, frivolous conversations, and time-wasting assignments.

Solution: Prepare for their sessions in an organized manner. Walking onto the court and winging it is a sure fire way to lose this student's respect. It's also meaningful to resist sharing your emotional baggage with this cognitive T design. They're not wired to deal with other's emotions. Staying on task with a systematic approach is highly appreciated by this brain design.

Challenge: ENTJ brain types are often seen as easy going, warm and friendly, and happy to engage with strangers. Once these athletes allow you in their inner circle, their true colors come out under stress. Parents and trusted entourage members get to see the colder, combative side of the TJ athlete.

Solution: Reestablish their control by asking them to take the leadership role in their training sessions. Redirect their drama from you against them, to their actions against their long-term goals. Typically, their drama is a result of their words not matching their actions.

Challenge: When overwhelmed, ENTJ personality profiles often misdirect their training regiments. They intuitively circle back to less important, comfortable drills and activities instead of fighting through the uncomfortable learning zone assignments.

Solution: Use the high school/college analogy, "You've already graduated from high school, Samantha. You don't have to repeat 9th grade over and over again. Let's stick to the higher education, tennis college curriculum!"

Challenge: ENTJ's are natural born leaders who prefer to control situations and the people surrounding them. Following isn't part of their DNA. ENTJ's often believe that their way is the only way.

Solution: Encourage ENTJ types to remain open to other people's vision because there is a significant skill to be able to listen and learn before dictating. To avoid seeming arrogant, remind them that they can learn more from listening than from shutting others down with a "know it all" attitude.

INTP: Introvert Intuitive Thinker Perceiver

Challenge: Like other NP's, focusing exclusively on mundane, repetitive tasks is often difficult. The same old boring routine day in day out is not the way to motivate this cerebral design. To them, it isn't seen as beneficial. It's seen as incompetent.

Solution: Since INTP's often find fundamental stroke repetition boring, challenge them early in the development of their software components. This brain design is extremely capable of multi-tasking throughout their sessions.

Challenge: INTP's usually prefer private lessons over group training. Too much "extroverting" is uncomfortable and draining to this profile. INTP's dislike being held responsible for other athlete's quality of work in team-oriented drill sessions.

Solution: Find time for private sessions. If private sessions are not possible, remind them that high-performance athletes have to learn to be comfortable when things get uncomfortable. This is a universal skill each profile has to master at the higher echelons of the sport.

Challenge: In the stress of competition, the intermediate INTP's have difficulty accessing their developed hardware. They often suffer from athletic "stage fright," typically due to the TP's future unrealistic thoughts of possible failure.

Solution: Anticipating failure falls into the underdeveloped component called emotional aptitude. "With intelligent risk comes reward" is a mantra I use if performance anxieties are derailing an athlete. Under stress, the INTP's often fall into the trap of avoiding their trained systems of "playing to win" as they unknowingly trade them in for a "play not to lose" system. Mastering any skill set, be it physical, mental, or emotional stems from skill immersion. So, the skills of "playing to win" stem from "playing to win" regardless of the day's outcome.

Challenge: Typically, INTP personalities are late bloomers when it comes to elegant strokes and smooth athleticism.

Solution: Incorporate yoga and Pilates type training to improve their gross motor skills, core strength, and balance. I find that INTP's can understand the coach's directives long before they can complete the athletic task. Patience from the coaches' corner pays off in spades because these athletes have great potential on the tennis court.

ENTP: Extrovert Intuitive Thinker Perceiver

Challenge: ENTP's are naturally born inventors. As their NP profiles shine, be cautious not to impose too many "Only do it my way" rigid rules in a micromanaging fashion.

Solution: Guide this personality profile gently as you encourage their creativeness in developing their unique style of play. Obviously, the laws of the game (physics and percentage shot selections) apply.

Challenge: ENTP's can cause havoc in group settings due to their enjoyment of confrontation. They are often natural-born warriors. If this type isn't nurtured correctly, they often fail to see others emotions as valid, so they frequently push teammates past their tolerance level. Since arguing is their strong suit, I encourage youngsters with this genetic predisposition to captain the school's debate team, in addition to their tennis.

Solution: Due to the mismanagement of others feelings, consider taking extra time to develop the emotional intelligence of this design. ENTP's are typically interested in new, abstract concepts and emotional intelligence is often intriguing to this type. This cognitive design finds learning new concepts fascinating.

Challenge: Intermediate ENTP's can often freeze in competition when their A-Plan is shut down. Performance anxiety symptoms of fear and panic appear when they can't believe they're failing. Performing without preset answers is highly uncomfortable with this design.

Solution: Success in competition requires the development of contingency plans. Wisely take the time to develop and rehearse A-Plans, B-Plans and even C-Plans. Once game plans are developed, ENTP's are quick thinkers with mental flexibility. The more strategies and tactics digested, the higher the confidence they will have in the flexibility in their performance.

Challenge: If these athletes believe they're going to get an ego-bruising loss, their pre-fabricated stress can turn into hypochondria. If the pressure of competition is too great in their minds, they are known to manifest ailments from head-to-toe to circumvent a poor performance. Excuses are designed and put into place before competition as a stress-reducing ego-out.

Solution: Obviously, I'm not a cognitive behavior therapist but working within the mental, emotional realm of high-performance tennis for over 30 years places me smack dab in the trenches. Needless to say, I have seen more of my fair share of invented ailments before competition. I suggest that the athlete redirect their focus from "I can't play... I've got a blister." to "Once the adrenaline kicks in, I won't even feel the blister." Redirecting their pessimistic thoughts makes the pain seem less significant. Countering their panic with controllable, performance goals will reassure the athlete and redirect their thoughts to a more optimist approach.

INTJ: Introvert Intuitive Thinker Judger

Challenge: INTJ's are often the stress heads of the club. Some seem to worry about almost everything. The undue stress arising from performance anxieties can derail even the best D-1 College players. It is critical that INTJ's understand that mental and emotional training will help them to relax in competition.

Solution: Like similar designs, the development of INTJ's software components should be a significant focal point in each training session. It's essential to incorporate the development of routines and rituals to assist them in managing their competitive emotions.

Challenge: Not unlike similar designs, a beginner or intermediate INTJ's stress level can skyrocket with having to perform in unfamiliar environments. Elements such as wind, shadows, excessive heat, even a different brand of tennis balls can send this cerebral design into an uncontrollable panic mode.

Solution: Whenever possible in practice, change the environment of their training sessions. Comfort in adapting stems from familiarity. Training should include the different ball spins, speeds and trajectories found in the varying styles of sparring partners. On tournament days, arrive a day early to familiarize the athlete with their new surroundings comfortably. Who does that, you ask? Federer, Nadal, Williams, Sharapova to name a few!

Challenge: A blessing and a curse of the INTJ personality profile is that they have well thought out lesson plans as a result of their IT dominant brain. Sadly, they fail to notify the coach of their perceived ideas. They then proceed to get upset when those ghost plans are ignored.

Solution: Coaches and parents should take the time to discuss daily training methods with their athlete. Lesson previews, as well as lesson reviews, are paramount when working with this brain design. Work together in meticulously planning this athlete's weekly list of training topics.

Challenge: INTJ's aren't the most elegant looking athletes yet can find great success on the tennis court if they're willing to put in the long hard work. Their natural born tendency is to systematically dissect the opponent's efficiencies and deficiencies and then drive their opponent nuts by only giving them what they hate.

Solution: Focus on developing their competitive tenacity. The beauty of this cerebral design is that they're genetically wired to be crafty mental game experts. Design tactical plays for each of the opponent's primary style of play from retrievers, to hard-hitting baseliners to net rushers. Expose the INTJ's terrifically effective counter punching skills as well as their enjoyment of watching their underdeveloped opponents implode.

CHAPTER 11: Assisting the 4 SJ Typographies
ESTJ, ISTJ, ISFJ, ESFJ

ESTJ- Extrovert Sensate Thinker Judger

Challenge: ESTJ's are an outgoing yet detail-oriented bunch. Asking them to perform in match play with a secondary system that hasn't been highly rehearsed is likely to cause them to freeze in their tracks.

Solution: Often, adaptations such as B or C game plans are needed in competition. Apply on-court and off-court sessions designed to develop their contingency plan. Serenity stems from confidence in a well-developed strategic plan.

Challenge: Due to their well thought out views, ESTJ's dislike incompetence and have issues with being accused of that trait.

Solution: Take extra time to design lesson plans. To them, "winging it" appears to be subpar. Instead of telling them what is wrong within the context of their performance, ask them what is wrong? Convince them in believing that they came up with the solution to the problem.

Challenge: ESTJ's carry more than their share of internal tension into competition. Under duress, their muscle groups often tighten under the weight of self-induced stress. Combine these inner demons with the highly charged emotional climate of competition, and it's common to watch them struggle at crunch time.

Solution: To perform while facing fear, introduce verbal and physical triggers they can rely on in between points. Customize verbal cheers such as "Let's Go! Right now! Fight!" And physical adrenaline pumping activities such as shadow swinging, moving feet and fist pumping.

Challenge: ESTJ's respond less to emotions and more to logic. Begging and pleading them to train efficiently doesn't fit into their brain design.

Solution: Replace being overly sympathetic with solution-based discussions. Explaining the analytics, the physics of the game, and the rationale behind the benefits of the exercise or percentages play is right up their alley.

ISTJ- Introvert Sensate Thinker Judger

Challenge: ISTJ's are not comfortable adapting and remaining flexible. Due to this factor, their single-mindedness is their greatest blessing and greatest curse.

Solution: Encourage ISTJ students to develop their secondary strokes and their contingency plans early on. If they don't build confidence in their approach shots, slices, short angles, and high and heavy strokes, they risk falling into a one-dimensional conservative, defensive ground-stroker.

Challenge: TJ types find it challenging to relax and enjoy the moment. To them, the tennis court is seen as a place of work and not play.

Solution: Inspire the belief that tournament competition is merely an information-gathering mission and not a life or death situation. ISTJ's would be well served to preset their generic (every day) plans and patterns as well as plans and patterns to pull different styles of opponents out of their comfortable systems of play.

Challenge: Frequent changes to their normal routines are often seen as unnecessarily rocking of the status quo. Change brings scary feelings such as fear, uncertainty, and self-doubt and ISTJ's resist such sensitivities.

Solution: Describe these inconsistent, unreliable feelings as calculated risks necessary to improve. Also, discuss the fact that remaining in one's comfort zone is illogical. It leaves the athlete in a state of limbo as their rivals continue to improve and leave them behind.

Challenge: ISTJ's are often perfectionists. In their mind, satisfaction only comes when a match is performed to perfection. Often these perfectionist types can build a 6-1, 3-0 lead, have one crummy game and to them, perfection is ruined; so they have a complete meltdown and complicate a routine victory.

Solution: Explain to perfectionist that even the very best perform excellently, not perfect. ATP stats reveal that Roger Federer and Novak Djokovic have won approximately 53% of the total points they play annually, and they have achieved #1 in the year-end rankings.

ISFJ- Introvert Sensate Feeler Judger

Challenge: Due to their feeler typography, ISFJ's typically have a difficult time with conflict, unfair gamesmanship and criticism. This leaves them more vulnerable on the emotional front.

Solutions: ISFJ's need positive feedback and lots of it. They perform best after solutions to handle confrontation are preset. This requires the coach to preset customized protocols ISFJ's can use in the face of unfair play. It would be wise to ask the student to spar while allowing the opponent to hook whenever the student hits the ball on the line. Role-playing their confrontational skills is essential.

Challenge: ISFJ's can become easily discouraged or depressed when reality doesn't meet their preconceived expectations. ISFJ's are often convinced that their thoughts are a reality. They often believe their pessimistic views of the future are absolutes versus mere assumptions.

Solution: Psychiatrists label speculations as cognitive distortions. Explain to the athlete that these embedded beliefs perpetuate future adverse actions that cause future failures. Because ISFJ's occasionally perceive reality inaccurately, they distort their very own feelings, thinking, and actions. Often, high-level coaching isn't about changing a stroke; it's about changing a mental state of mind.

Challenge: The ISFJ athletes are typically gifted athletically, but if their emotional components are left underdeveloped, ISFJ's perform fearful, apprehensive, and often fold in the face of confrontation.

Solution: Due to the combination of shared stress, and companionship, ISFJ's seem to perform best in doubles. If they can get over the possibility of letting their partner down, they leave their conservative, timid persona behind and rise to the occasion. In singles, ISFJ's dislike center stage so keeping them out of the limelight helps to reduce stress. While defensive and safe by nature, these athletic individuals should be educated and motivated to apply controlled aggression in competition.

Challenge: ISFJ's are often found spending the majority of their time grooving bad habits on the practice court instead of simply asking the coach for assistance. It is often uncomfortable for them to ask for help. To their detriment, they prefer to blend-in instead of stand-out. Their need for harmony usually exceeds their personal need for success on the tennis court.

Solution: Encourage the athlete to communicate three topics for improvement before each session. After the session, make time to discuss their feelings regarding their progress. Gently remind them that winning requires the ability to put themselves first, applying "in your face" willingness to fight in the face of confrontation.

ESFJ- Extrovert Sensate Feeler Judger

Challenge: Young ESFJ's can lean heavily on their J brain design and believe it is their obligation to point out others who aren't following the rules. As they mature, they're typically nurtured to avoid such confrontations. In a 10 & Under Tennis class, it's not uncommon to hear an eight-year-old ESFJ say, "Coach Frank, Joeys not doing it right over on court 12!"

Solution: It's meaningful to explain to these athletes that they're attending tennis classes for a specific purpose and that is to improve their skill sets at the quickest rate possible. Extra-curricular activities like monitoring other attendees' behavior or putting socialization above training aren't in their best interest.

Challenge: Taking a drill sergeant coaching approach doesn't work well with this sensitive type. The old school problem-oriented methodology of coaching will only serve to make the athlete feel tense and overstressed.

Solution: Due to their EF brain design, it's recommended to motivate through optimism. Point out what they're doing correctly before suggesting to fine tune a problem area. Commend them for their efforts and employ five positive comments to each one negative comment.

Challenge: ESFJ's can get too caught up in their social status, rankings and others opinions about themselves. This preoccupation can stunt their actual development as they chase ranking points instead of chasing improvement.

Solution: Provide time sensitive improvement goals weekly. Having goal dates motivates the athlete to complete objectives that help them make their aspirations become their reality.

Challenge: Due to their loyal nature, ESFJ's typically need plenty of quality time with friends and family. Issues arise because EF types often put the needs of others ahead of their own. This is seen when non-athletic friends consistently pull them away from their practice schedule to socialize.

Solution: With the athlete, sit and organize their weekly developmental plan including time to socialize. Their SJ functional typography would benefit from time management as they structure their time to accommodate both tennis and socialization.

CHAPTER 12: Physical Skills Versus Life Skills

Marcus is a gifted tennis player from Phoenix, Arizona. At 16 he possesses incredible athleticism. He's 6'3" and is ripped. His speed, agility, and stamina are off the charts. His tennis specific skills are also above average. He possesses a huge serve and a killer forehand. Marcus's UTR is hovering around 10.8. College coaches recruiting should be salivating for him, but sadly for Marcus and his folks, tennis scholarships are not being offered.

The red flags that the experienced college coaches quickly identify are underdeveloped character traits and life skills. You see, Marcus can't communicate with others, and when he does, a storm of pessimism engulfs everyone around him like a dark cloud. As for his life skills, the college coaches quickly pick up on the fact that he's late for their meetings, unorganized, and blames others for his downfalls. On-court Marcus shows irrational anger, reckless shot selections, and a lack of perseverance, adaptability, and resiliency even in practice match play. Due to Marcus's underdeveloped software, his D-1 College dreams won't be coming true. It's within the job description of coaches and parents to teach positive character traits and life skills along with their tennis skill sets.

High-performance tennis is the combination of four required skill sets: character skills, life skills, athleticism, and tennis-specific skills. Customized training focuses on all four of these components, however, the degree of focus is based on the athlete's specific needs. It is the job description of a progressive coach to navigate the mastery of all four of these skills effectively.

1) Character Skills

Character skills are productive personality traits. These habits include empathy, interpersonal skills for communicating and interacting effectively with others, a positive-optimistic attitude, ethics, morals, and leadership traits.

2) Life Skills

Life skills are defined as the abilities to thrive within the challenges of an athlete's everyday life. These include cognitive skills for analyzing performance and personal skills for organizing developmental plans and managing oneself.

3) Athletic Skills

Athletic skills are defined as the physical qualities that are characteristic of well-rounded athletic individuals regardless of the sport. Athletic skills include upper and lower body strength, fitness, stamina, speed, core balance, and agility.

4) Tennis Skills

Tennis skills are the particular skill sets that define a high performance-tennis specific athlete. Experts in this field possess a complete tool belt of strokes, tactics, strategies and of course, emotional aptitude to compete at the higher echelons of the game.

I work primarily with nationally, and ITF ranked juniors, college athletes, and young touring professionals. Athletes at this level are successful due to their skills management. In my world of high-performance athletes, stats are important because they help customize the athlete's training regimen.

In regards to stats, the following are the typical percentages ratios of physical skills to life skills that I have witnessed throughout the three primary stages of junior tennis. I'm convinced that positive character traits and customized life skills development hold the secret key to maximizing athletic potential.

At Ages: 7-11, junior athletes I work with possess:

- 10%: Medium physical talent, medium desire, medium commitment.
- 40%: Medium physical talent, maximum desire, maximum commitment.
- 10%: Gifted physically, maximum desire, maximum commitment.
- 40%: Gifted physically, no desire, no commitment.

In this introductory stage, there is nothing more heartbreaking than the estimated 40% of gifted athletes I see with zero desire or work ethic (AKA life skills.)

At Ages: 12-15, junior athletes I work with possess:

- 25%: Medium physical talent, medium desire, medium commitment.
- 45%: Medium physical talent, maximum desire, maximum commitment.
- 5%: Gifted physically, maximum desire, maximum commitment.
- 25%: Gifted physically, no desire, no commitment.

In this developmental stage, the medium talented athletes with customized developmental plans and well-nurtured life skills begin to shine. Simultaneously the gifted athletes with poor nurturing, and life skills development are dropping out.

At Ages: 16-18, junior athletes I work with possess:

- 10%: Medium physical talent, medium desire, medium commitment.
- 70%: Medium talent, maximum desire, maximum commitment.
- 20%: Gifted physically, maximum desire, maximum commitment.
- 0%: Gifted physically, no desire, no commitment.

At the top of the junior tennis food chain, life skills trump physical talent.

The outcomes (wins and rankings) are contingent on how well the parents and coaches deliver the four skill sets and how adept the athlete is at assimilating this information.

As youth sports researchers often say, "Life skills are purposely taught, not hopefully caught."

The following chapters will identify the hidden benefits of life skills and character building. Life skills and positive character traits are essential elements found in *The Soft Science of Tennis*.

CHAPTER 13: Why Character Building Matters

Jenny's a full-time student at the First Strike Tennis Academy in Southern California and has been for nine years. In her own words: "I'm stuck, I'm SCTA ranked in the upper 80's and going nowhere fast." Jenny's father is also frustrated with her tennis because he knows Jenny is a gifted athlete and he feels her academy is letting her down, despite the incredible amount of money he shells out to them each month. Jenny and her father both believe she is capable of achieving better results.

The coaching staff at First Strike had convinced Jenny that she was doing everything she was supposed to do and to be patient and she would see results soon. Jenny confided in me that her motivation was gone and she was ready to hang up her rackets. She then broke down in tears as she revealed that although she's good in practice, in competition her competitive grit, patience, and effort have abandoned her. She looked down and sobbed, "I'm just so tired of being average." Jenny's father interrupted and confessed, booking this session with you was our last resort."

It didn't take long to uncover the White Elephant on the court, which was the fact that Jenny has been training inefficiently for almost a decade.

Our initial conversation began with me asking Jenny some fundamental tennis developmental questions. "Since you're telling me you know all too well how to be average, let me ask you an opposing question: Can you tell me how not to be average?" Jenny said, "Um...to do more training than my peers?" I smiled and said, "What's even more important than the quantity of training?" "I don't know... the quality of the training?" she responded. I agreed wholeheartedly. I then asked Jenny what she thought the difference was between group drilling and a customized developmental plan. "Well," she said. "I guess a customized developmental plan focuses on individual needs versus group activities. I said, "Right again sister!"

I asked Jenny about her tennis goals. She perked up and said, "It used to be to play D-1 Tennis at Stanford but …" "Ok, great!" I jumped in. "Now what is your customized weekly plan to make it a reality? What are you doing week-in and week -out that is setting you far apart from your peers?" … (Crickets) "Let me ask you another way, has your only training been in the academy format? …More silence. I gave it the dramatic one minute pause, which to her must have felt like an hour.

I sat back, took a deep breath, and said, "I see the problem. Jenny, you don't have a customized plan. A goal without a customized plan isn't a goal at all …it's simply a dream." I explained to Jenny that everyone has dreams, but a dream isn't going to come true without a specific weekly customized developmental plan. Jenny's eye's brightened, and I saw her beautiful smile for the first time.

"I believe you owe it to yourself to attack your tennis development from a new perspective. Let's hit a few balls so I can see your strokes and movement."

So we hit a few baskets of balls as I identified her strengths and weaknesses in her primary and secondary strokes. We then sat down and went to work designing her customized weekly planner based on her efficiencies and deficiencies within her four main components: strokes, athleticism, mental and emotional. Our evaluation session was a mind-blowing revelation to Jenny and her Dad. No one had ever actually dissected Jenny's game, let alone provided customized solutions for improvement. Our first day together went by quickly as we evaluated and improved her tennis IQ, her emotional aptitude, her organizational skills and we made adjustments in her deficient coaching entourage.

Jenny didn't need to groove her stationary strokes or to run more laps around the track. She needed to apply life skills, positive character traits and a renewed belief in herself. Throughout our few days together, I identified the direction of training required and simply motivated her to be accountable for organizing her very own training regimen. She applied solid character traits such as the determination to devise an innovative, customized weekly blueprint. She was open-minded and humble throughout our sessions. Strong character traits are needed to champion tennis and life.

Within six months of completely modifying her training regimen, life skills, and positive character traits Jenny achieved a top 10 SCTA ranking and went on to play D-1 College ball. (The names have been changed to protect the guilty).

Building character in young athletes is essential to the success of the athlete on and off the court. Positive character not only assists the athletes on the court but guides them as they make the world a better place. An excellent character is a secret precursor of winning. It drives performance, which accelerates results. It's the heartbeat of *The Soft Science of Tennis.* Sadly, in today's generation, many parents assume that the coaches are teaching positive character traits and critical life skills, while coaches believe that it's the parents who are educating these essential skills and sadly it's a missing link in developing athletes.

"Excellent character is the secret precursor of winning. It drives consistent training which accelerates results."

Character counts, so what is character? It's a combination of the athlete's emotional qualities, beliefs, and values. Great character isn't a genetic predisposition. Humans aren't born with great character. Good character is a learned skill set with well nurtured emotional enhancements. One's character, good or bad shines in all its glory when the athlete competes and under duress. Developing character molds the athlete's inner dialog, which either pumps them up or tears them down on a daily basis.

"The underlining effectiveness of a parent or coach lies in their ability to develop positive character skills."

The Power of Choice

Positive character motivates the athlete to forge ahead. Negative character allows the athlete to give up. A critical question in our sport is "How do we teach our athletes to handle losses?"

A modern term used in sports psychology is Posttraumatic Growth (PTG). Psychologists apply the term PTG to describe a positive psychological change that can result from a traumatic experience, such as athletic failure. Though losing may not seem like a tragic event to some, to others competitive losses can be mentally and emotionally crippling. PTG methodologies help clients through difficult situations by encouraging them to take responsibility with the power of choice.

The athlete can choose to fight or retreat. Tennis champions actually lose and lose often throughout their career. The athletes who choose to use their scar tissue as motivation to fight and endure the athletic pressure persevere and reach the top. Admirable character opens up the athlete to forge ahead instead of shutting down and giving up.

"You need to develop a thick skin" is a common mantra for strong character building. It's an effective defense to the critics. Trust me, the most common way you know you're rising above the crowd is when others begin to trash-talk and criticize you solely because of their petty jealousy. If athletes aren't able to take criticism, they should stay home, lie on the couch and stop improving immediately!"

In regards to character, actions speak louder than words. Parents and coaches need to remember that they are modeling character and that their actions have a more significant impact than their words. It is the role of parents and coaches to create a positive environment for ideal character building. Build character and lead by example:

- It's cool to be kind so choose kindness.
- Vulnerability is a courageous character trait and not a weakness. So embrace vulnerability.
- Share successes and failures. Share your story as a learning tool.
- Laugh and joke as you apply humor to your daily training sessions.
- Give credit to others for your success.
- Compliment others daily on everything and anything.

"Invest more time and energy in your positive character building, and you'll witness your athletes modeling positive behavior."

Character Traits

Character and a solid moral compass are part of the athlete's foundation, which dictates behavior and facilitates success. The same is true for a successful coaching business; the character traits found in a champion are the same character traits that provide the foundation of a sustainable business.

20 Essential Character Traits Worth Educating

Print the following 20 Essential Character Traits and review with your athlete. Discuss how each trait affects their personal tennis development.

1) **Motivation**: The reason or reasons for attaining your goals.

2) **Trustworthiness**: The ability to be relied on as honest or truthful.

3) **Gratitude**: The appreciation of actions and benefits bestowed upon you.

4) **Accountability**: The condition of being responsible for your actions.

5) **Commitment**: The position of being dedicated to your cause.

6) **Respectfulness**: A curious regard for others feelings or situation.

7) **Grit**: Strength of character; courage and resolve.

8) **Integrity**: Having a strong moral compass and principles.

9) **Innovative**: Applying creative problem solving and advanced thinking.

10) **Competency**: The ability to perform efficiently and successfully.

11) **Honesty**: Acting with fairness and righteous conduct.

12) **Loyalty**: A strong feeling of support or allegiance to your supporters.

13) **Ethics**: The morals and principles that govern your behavior.

14) **Patience**: The capacity to tolerate delay or suffering without getting upset.

15) **Desire**: A deep feeling of acquiring something or wishing for it to happen.

16) **Effort**: The amount of energy put into an attempt.

17) **Sincerity**: The quality of being free from pretense and deceit.

18) **Open-Mindedness**: The willingness to consider new ideas without prejudice.

19) **Unselfishness**: The desire to accept the needs of others before your own.

20) **Humble**: Showing a modest estimate of your importance.

So does the participation in sports help build praiseworthy character traits? Yes, but an athlete's character must be first introduced, nurtured, and developed by parents and coaches. The essential character traits demonstrated on-court in competition were first gained off-court. These traits were nurtured by choice ...not by chance.

CHAPTER 14: Life Skills Maximize Athletic Development

While at the Easter Bowl Championships a parent came up to me and said "You're the Tennis Parent Bible guy, right? I have your books, but I've got to say, I hate everything about junior tennis. I hate the tournament directors, the insane hours, the cost of equipment, the crazy travel schedule, and the lessons are a waste of time. My daughter's coaches aren't teaching her a stinking thing. She just lost second round again this year!"

I politely waited for her to take a breath and we began a conversation:

Frank: *"Hi... Yes, I'm Frank. What's your name?"*
Kathryn: *"I'm Kathryn," she said as she crossed her arms in front of her.*
Frank: *"Hi Kathryn. I have about 30 minutes before my player's match. Can we chat for a few minutes?" Kathryn rolled her eyes, so I immediately asked, "Your daughter is obviously a very talented player to be playing the Easter Bowl. Can you think of a handful of reasons you could be grateful?"*
Kathryn: *"No... Not a one!" She barked.*
Frank: *"Kathryn, what's your daughter's ranking?"*
Kathryn: *"Oh, around 30 in the Nation."*
Frank: *"Top 30 in the Country is outstanding! Isn't that something both you and your daughter should be proud of?"*
Kathryn: *"I mean...I guess so."*
Frank: *"Has she been offered a full-ride college scholarship?"*
Kathryn: *"Yes, of course! She has about a dozen schools courting her, but she is only interested in USC."*
Frank: *"Now that's something to be grateful for- a dozen D-1 Universities wanting your daughter to play for them!"*
Kathryn: *"Well...that's true."*

Frank: "I bet you guys have seen some cool parts of the world as she has competed in National and ITF tennis events."

Kathryn: "Oh yes! We've been throughout the country, the Caribbean, the Middle East, Canada, and Europe."

Frank: "Aren't you grateful for that time together with your daughter?"

Kathryn: "Yes, I am... and we did have great fun on those trips."

Frank: "Can you tell me about the life lessons learned from participating in the sport?"

Kathryn: "What do you mean?"

Frank: "You know... time management, resiliency, and organizational skills to name a few?"

Kathryn: "You're right. There have been so many life lessons and blessings that have come from playing this game."

Frank: "Kathryn, the healthiest of all emotions is gratitude, and in 5 minutes you just revealed so much to be grateful for... and there's plenty more if you choose to look in the right direction."

Kathryn: "I needed that pep talk. Can I give you a hug?"

We have all heard that sports teach life skills, but did you know the opposite is also true? Well nurtured life skills and character improves athletic potential at a quicker rate.

"Life skills improve the developmental plan which in-turns skyrocket athletic potential."

World class coaches and parents must intentionally see life skills as essential attributes that need to be acquired, practiced, and perfected in and out of the athletic arena. Being equipped with life skills will not only improve the athlete's competitive match performance but will inevitably have a positive effect on the sustainability of their customized developmental plans.

Obviously, well-developed life skills are highly transferable to other areas of the athletes' lives. It is important to note that the vast majority of tennis athletes do not partake in competitive tennis as a lifelong career. However, the following list of essential life skills will last a lifetime, enabling them to evolve successfully into the next phase of their life.

Life Skills Development

Parents and coaches, I highly encourage setting aside time to increase your athlete's mental toughness and emotional aptitude. Arrange a classroom session or non-hitting homework assignment weekly. Ask each serious-minded student to Google or YouTube, the following 20 essential life skills and draft a paragraph describing their customized developmental plan to improve each skill.

Time Management

The time management life skill is the ability to use one's time efficiently or productively. A successful athlete with strong time management skills would organize daily, weekly, and monthly planners to assist in scheduling the development of each of the four major components (technical, athletic, mental, and emotional) essential to compete at the higher levels.

Adaptability

The adaptability life skill is being able to adjust to different situations and conditions comfortably. To get the most from your physical talent, one must be open to change. Adapting is emotional intelligence at work.

"No athlete has ever reached their full potential without learning to overcome stress, fear, and discomfort. Life skills are essential."

Handling Adversity

Handling adversity is a critical athletic and life skill. Competition brings hardship, drama, and suffering along with the positive attributes. Overcoming daily problems is a driving force of champions. Seeing adversity as a challenge versus a life or death crisis is vital.

Handling Stress

Stress causes physiological and mental tension. It occurs when one believes that their physical skills aren't strong enough to meet the challenge. While some personalities stress more than others, proper preparation and a positive attitude dramatically reduce stress levels.

Perseverance

Perseverance is one's ability to stay on course through setbacks, discouragement, injuries, and losses. It is the ability to fight stubbornly to achieve greatness.

"The most meaningful lessons come from the toughest losses…If the student is willing to listen."

Courage

Courage is the ability to apply belief in your skills in spite of the threat at hand. A courageous athlete knows that competition in sports is to be embraced and not feared. Courage is not allowing oneself to listen to the typical noise of "What if I lose?"

Work Ethic

Work ethic is a diligent, consistent standard of conduct. Strengthening physical, mental and emotional components and the attainment of goals is dependent on a deliberate customized plan and hard work.

Resiliency

Resiliency is the capacity to recover and adjust to difficulties. Champions fall, hurt and fail just like us, but they have preset protocols to adapt and press on. Winners aren't always the most intelligent or even the strongest athletes in the event. They are often the individuals who respond with the best adjustments after misfortunes.

"Great performances stem from a peaceful heart. So after mistakes, forgive yourself quickly."

Goal Setting

Goal setting is the process of identifying something that you want to accomplish with measurable goals. Dreams are a great start, but the work begins when both specific performance improvement goals and outcome goals have action plans and target dates. Setting daily, monthly and long-term goals build the emotional strength you seek.

Sticking to Commitments

Commitments are obligations that restrict freedom of action. Staying loyal to a written action plan separates the champion from the part-time hobbyist. Hobbyists train when it's convenient. Committed athletes put their sport above their social calendar.

Determination

Determination is the power to persist with a singular fixed purpose. Champions are stubbornly tenacious to reach their goals. Champions often begin as average athletes with abnormal determination.

Problem-Solving Skills

Identifying the problem is only the first step. Step two is to isolate the causes of the problem. Step three is then to customize the solution to the problem. Creative problem solving requires digging deeper rather than merely identifying the flaw.

"When dealing with gamesmanship, mature athletes do not give the drama more importance then intelligently remaining on script."

Spotting Patterns and Tendencies

Patterns and tendencies are an individual's predisposition to act repeatedly. Spotting reoccurring behavior is essential to understanding your strengths and weaknesses as well as defeating a worthy opponent.

Discipline

Discipline is behavior that is judged by how well it follows a set of rules. It is one of the most important emotional elements that turn dreams and goals into accomplishments. It often requires you to choose to train when you'd rather be socializing. Discipline is painful but not nearly as painful as losing to people you should be beating.

Sportsmanship

Sportsmanship is the underlying respect for the game, the rules governing the sport, the opponents and the officials. It's giving it your all and playing with confidence and pride regardless of the outcome.

Focus

Focus is the ability to centralize your attention. Examples include adhering to short-term goals, such as a single play, point or game, all the way towards attaining long-term goals, such as playing a junior Grand Slam or being offered a college athletic scholarship.

"Improving involves cleaning out the clutter. Adding more isn't always the answer. Often, solutions stem from doing less."

Preparation Skills

The life skill of being prepared is especially important in athletics. Preparing properly for battle is one of the most neglected aspects of intermediate athletes. Success begins with total preparation. It is indeed the key to preventing a poor performance.

Persistence

Persistence is the continued passion for action in spite of opposition. You need constant energy devoted to your sport, anything less means that you're a hobbyist. Persistence gets you to the top. Consistency with that persistent frame of mind keeps you there.

"Don't confuse busy work with productive growth. Practice in the manner you are expected to perform."

Dedication

Dedication is the quality of being committed to a purpose. Dedication to a sport requires passion and commitment to strive for daily improvement. Lazy, non-athletic people use the word "obsessed" to describe the dedicated athletes.

Positive Self-Image

Strong emotional aptitude starts with positive self-esteem. Trusting yourself is a key to competing freely. Changing the negative self-talk into positive internal dialog is a great start.

"Strong competitive character at crunch time stems from life lessons developed."

The following chapter uncovers the importance of nurturing and motivating athletes, which involves changing negative attitudes and the unhealthy mental habits that are keeping them from reaching their potential.

CHAPTER 15: The Importance of Nurturing

A family from Georgia called to book a 3-day customized evaluation session with me in California. Steven, the dad, was a former nationally ranked junior and top college player. Eddy, his 14-year-old son, is a junior competitor. As we began our tennis evaluation, within minutes, I noticed some glaring red flags. Halfway through the morning session, I could tell that Steven wanted Eddy to be a tennis star much more than Eddy.

A lack of athleticism wasn't the cause of Eddy's failings in tournament competition. I realized rather quickly what was keeping Eddy from attaining the results he was capable of achieving. Although Eddy was a talented ball striker, he needed a customized development plan to develop the skills essential to becoming an elite athlete.

In our afternoon session, after we bonded a bit, I asked Eddy, "Bro, What are your tennis goals? Where do you see yourself in four years?" Eddy responded, "I don't know. I mean, I'll give it a try...if it works out then great. Fed's life doesn't look too shabby. I guess I could be a pro like Roger."

Eddy's common lackadaisical approach showed interest in the game but lacked commitment, and there's a big difference between interest and commitment. Athletes merely interested in the sport, train when they feel like it. They train when it conveniently fits into their social calendar. I asked Eddy what was holding him back. Eddy said, "I don't know...I just don't always feel like training." I added that's fair because you've got to commit to it, to believe in it." The seed was planted. I simply needed to let it blossom within.

At lunch, I asked Steven if he thought Eddy was committed to excellence. He hesitated and then said, "No but that's why I brought him cross-country to you. I hear that you're great at motivating excellence and nurturing that commitment."

While evaluating Eddy's hardware (strokes and athleticism) with on-court drills, I began the positive brainwashing process of nurturing his commitment. I reminded Eddy that he had mentioned that his buddy's at home were all top 20 in his section. "Yeah, and I'm tired of losing early every tournament and being their stupid cheerleader," I asked him if he thought he was doing all he could to be the best tennis player possible. He responded, "No, probably not…"

All too often naive athletes want the rewards to materialize before the hard work takes place. I mentioned to Eddy several times throughout our three-day evaluation that being committed to excellence means that if he wanted to join his buddies in the top 20, he would have to prioritize his tennis above his social life. Athletes have to train like a world class athlete for years before they ever reach world-class status. I then threw out a couple of goofy life analogies: "You've got to chop the wood and build a fire before you feel the heat, right? You've got to prepare the soil, plant the seed and work the fields before you can harvest the crop", right?" Before I could throw out another annoying analogy, Eddy interrupted.

"Yeah, yeah I get it. There are two approaches: Commitment to excellence or acceptance of mediocrity." "Right! And either way, you've got to live with your decision." I replied. At that moment, I sensed that the light bulb went off in his head. I've got an idea, "Let's work through it together and commit for 3-months. After 3-months, if it isn't working for you, then you're free to chill and play the sport as a hobby. Give the 100% commitment a shot. I bet that if you put in the effort and stick to your customized developmental plan week in and week out, you'll transform into a top 20 player by year's end!"

Six weeks later I got a text from Eddy with a photo of him holding up his first USTA trophy. All it said was, "I just had to climb the mountain…then I was able to see the view. Thanks, Coach!"

Developmental Psychology

"It is not nature versus nurture; it is nature and nurture."

Today there's a movement called Developmental Psychology. These experts research the intertwining relationship between genetic and environmental influences. In regards to the athletes' environmental influences, the two most important influences I've witnessed are their parents and coaches. Teachers and older siblings come in a close second. We influence why athletes think the way they think, why they say what they say and why they do what they do. We are the environmental influences that mold their talents and temperaments.

Developmental Psychology researchers use the word plasticity as they discover deeper implications to how humans respond to nurturing. Following are two negative pre-match preparation pep talks given to an athlete's by his parents. Although both messages lack positive support, it is the way in which the athlete chooses to respond that is interesting.

Toxic Pre Match Parental Pep Talk

"Joseph, if you blow it again this weekend, your mother and I are considering pulling the plug on your tennis. I'll be taking notes and listing all your shortcomings on my iPad. Don't blow it! Love, Dad."

Uninvolved Parent Pre Match Dialog

"Joey, honey… Mommy's driving into the city to Nordstrom's half-yearly sale. I have to drop you off at 7:00 a.m. I put lunch money in your bag. Enjoy your little game. I'll pick you up between 6:00 p.m. and 7:00 p.m. Mommy."

Although the first pep talk is clearly negative and soul-wrenching to read let alone experience, the second pep talk is just as negative. A parent that takes no interest in their child's passion is showing a lack of support and encouragement. Remember, it's how the athlete chooses to respond that's critical. Some athletes work hard to prove their parents right. Some fight all their lives to prove their parents wrong. Which of the following responses would you choose?

Response A-The Athletes folds as they feel the lack of parental confidence, love, and support and shortly quit the game. Proving the parents right.

Response B- The athlete applies plasticity as they use their parent's horrendous pre-match pep talks to motivate better performance. Proving the parents wrong.

Self-Nurturing

I believe that high-performance athletes determined to be the best they can be, have to take nurturing to another level. I call it self-nurturing, and I believe it to be the most important life skill. Self-nurturing is choosing to apply persistence and resiliency in the face of poor outside influences. I've witnessed athletes with incredible coaching and parenting

126

who choose to fail, as well as, athletes with absolutely pitiful coaching and parenting who choose to succeed.

If success is in the athlete's blood, I suggest motivating them to think of the negative people and their words as fuel. Proving someone wrong who doesn't believe in them is powerful motivation. It's self-nurturing at its finest. These individuals make the athlete work smarter, harder and longer …all for the reward of proving them wrong. Revenge is funny that way.

Improving self-nurturing skills requires us to put aside our ego and listen to others. I'm not suggesting that you agree with 100% of what they're saying, but rather consider the context of their words and take a look in the mirror and decide if there's any truth to their comments. Every one of us has aspects of our life that we can improve.

Coaches, parents, and athletes with a little self-reflection, we can all challenge ourselves in the realm of self-nurturing. To me, self-nurturing is a daily self-educating process. Every industry leader I admire is obsessed with self-improvement. They research relentlessly, attend conferences, read, write books, and take online courses to continue to learn and improve. They expose their deficiencies and make them efficiencies.

"The great self-nurturers of our time are growth mindset individuals who see futuristically, something greater that is currently present."

CHAPTER 16: Overriding Negative Past Belief Systems

It was September 1986, after my second stint at teaching tennis at the Wooster College Summer Tennis Camps. I decided that I wanted to give full-time tennis teaching a real shot. I'd been trapped in Ohio's nonstop rain watching a PBS television series called Future Sports. There on my TV, I watched a young Vic Braden combine standup comedy with the most intriguing sports science I'd ever heard. This short, pudgy tennis teacher with a contagious smile was light years ahead of any tennis instruction I'd ever seen. If I were to impact my clients, I'd first have to be a student of the game and improve my tennis IQ, and for that, I would need a real mentor.

I arrived in Southern California, drove past Cooks Corner, a Harley biker bar that's still going strong today, and continued driving up El Toro, for what seemed to be a never-ending road, straight to Coto De Caza. I knocked on the office door of the famous Vic Braden Tennis College. "Hi, I'm Frank. I want to learn how to coach this game. I'm a decent player and have a knack for people." Mary Lay, The Tennis College Director, said, in the sweetest voice, "Well, we have a full staff, and we get about a dozen great resumes a week but if you want to take notes and observe Vic and the staff you're welcome here!"

So, every day for the next two weeks I arrived at the tennis college at 8:00 a.m. and left the gates around 6:00 p.m. all the while intently observing and taking six legal pads full of notes. Fourteen days later, I was offered a job coaching at this prestigious tennis school called The Vic Braden Tennis College (VBTC). I guess they saw that the new 23-year-old kid was persistent and hungry for knowledge.

I couldn't have been happier being paid to continue to learn while I taught. It was at this time when I discovered how emotionally inept I was... A VBTC seasoned coach placed a handheld cassette tape recorder under my teaching basket. He said it would be meaningful for me to tape a session and to listen to the recording and count how many positive to negative comments I had made. In a one hour recording, I was horrified and humiliated to admit that I said "Don't do this, don't do that" 49 times! ...And I thought I was helping! If I could find that poor couple today, I'd gladly refund them their money. I wanted to be so positive and helpful, but my past belief systems came out in all its negative glory. It was a life-changing, soul-crushing lesson I needed to learn. My pessimistic past was influencing my coaching.

Ironically, as I had observed Vic coaching, I felt a kindred spirit (We were both ENFP's), and I knew I was in the right place. My genetic predisposition had always been to be kind and personable. Observing Vic validated my intuition that his positive view of the world was a better fit for me personally.

During my first year of teaching at the VBTC, I worked continuously to override my negative past beliefs and exposed my true positive genetic predisposition. My childhood experiences molded my inner beliefs, and these subconscious, pessimistic character traits didn't sit well with me. Vic, and his wife Melody and the kind tennis college staff encouraged me daily with the power of choice. They helped me turn my scars into praiseworthy character. Interestingly, they did so much more than teach me how to teach the game. They taught me how to change from a pessimist to an optimist, and I owe the world to them. Fortunately for me, I was able to open and direct Vic Braden Tennis Colleges, represent Vic as his agent and most importantly, become lifelong friends.

Reprogramming a Negative Athletes Brain

It's within the parents and coaches job description to help change the way negative personalities see themselves and the world around them. Often, like my younger self; athletes harbor past oppressive patterns of belief. These false beliefs are their perceptions of the truth and they are often based on the distorted knowledge that is likely holding them back.

Negative believers typically have a fixed mindset versus growth mindset. Fixed mindset individuals stubbornly believe that individuals can't really grow, learn and improve. A common false fixed mindset belief is "Some are born with it... some just aren't."

Psychologists refer to the subconscious knowledge (negative thoughts) we form as young children as conditioned beliefs. These pessimistic beliefs are developed with the help of parents, friends, social media, teachers, coaches and society. All of these influencers mold the athlete's thoughts and actions. Without a conscious effort to question whether or not these beliefs are helpful, many children unknowingly take these conditioned beliefs into adulthood.

Believing the negative perceptions of others can destroy an athlete's inner belief (dialog) and override intelligent self-coaching under stressful match conditions. Negative past beliefs become the athlete's self-fulfilling prophecy. Athletes young and old often believe what their authority figure tells them, such as:

- You're not talented enough.
- You're not smart enough.
- You lost in your first three events. Try another sport.
- You're too short; you're too slow.
- You're too young; you're too old.

It is essential that parents, coaches, and mentors learn to teach optimism, regardless of their personal conditioned beliefs to maximize the potential in their children and athletes. Though not every athlete is capable of or may not even desire to become a high-performance player, it is essential that every athlete is given the opportunity a growth mindset affords. When nurtured correctly, one day these children will be able to influence others positively.

Destroying Negative Past Beliefs

Educate Choices

The old saying is "It's not the event that shapes us, it's how we choose to view it." After competition, it is not healthy to focus on everything the athlete did wrong. Growth-minded individuals choose to focus on opportunities that lead to physical, emotional, mental and spiritual growth.

Replace Negative Perceptions with Positive Affirmations

Past and present pessimistic beliefs shape an athlete's current opinions. List their negative perceptions and discuss where they originated. Then assist the athlete in rewriting their inner dialog with positive versions to reprogram the athlete's beliefs. Coaches, parents, and athletes, please realize that overriding and rewiring a pessimistic outlook is a very doable task given time and patience.

Educate Cognitive Dissonance

Cognitive dissonance refers to the athlete's inconsistent opposing thoughts and beliefs. It's the natural mental discomfort or psychological stress that comes with change. Replacing an old belief with a new belief is similar to reprogramming a flawed stroke. Typically, it takes 4-6 weeks for the new motor program to override the old flawed stroke.

At the beginning of the metamorphosis, the athlete owns two opposite belief systems, the old and the new. The older more comfortable version will initially overtake and resist the new. This inner war should be explained to any student suffering from their past negatives beliefs.

The time it takes to replace their disempowering belief with their new empowering belief is customized to the time and effort the individual puts into the metamorphosis. Some athletes will choose to speed up the optimistic priming process with hours of neuro priming per week, while other less committed athletes may only choose to set aside one hour a week. Obviously, the time dedicated to the project dictates the speed and effectiveness of the transformation.

Neuro Priming the New Belief System

Together the parent/coach and athlete should sit down and list the benefits of the new optimistic belief system. The athlete should be encouraged to read their list of positive affirmations list into their voice recorder app on their cell phone and listen to their recordings nightly to Neuro Prime (visualize and mentally rehearse) their optimistic beliefs. Negative past beliefs can be destroyed and replaced. Optimistic beliefs begin with the athletes vividly imagining themselves performing to perfection in competition. Persistence is key as the new empowering beliefs gain control and the disempowering beliefs die out.

"Thought patterns shape our lives and help or hinder athletic performance."

Overriding my negative past beliefs 32 years ago contributed significantly to my change and success as a teacher, author, and human being. Re-conditioning a negative athlete is one of the most satisfying experiences a coach will ever experience.

Once the athlete becomes aware of their limiting perceptions, and they choose to destroy their negative inner dialog, they will recognize the unnecessary pain that has been holding them back. It's incredibly gratifying to witness a struggling athlete blossom into a confident, optimistic, happier person.

While coaches and even some **parents** routinely spot flawed strokes, most allow their athletes negative self-dialog to go unchecked. Overriding the athletes past pessimistic belief system is a critical function in *The Soft Science of Tennis*.

Perception Awareness

Often, athletes listen to that little pessimistic voice inside their brain all day long. This internal conversation programs their attitude, effort and of course, their match behavior. In this case, shifting attention from stroke adjustments to an attitude adjustment is mandatory. Erasing by replacing negative voices with positive ones is essential.

"In the heat of battle, positive versus negative internal dialog is what often separates the winners from losers."

The following is a list of positive personality traits that I suggest nurturing on a daily basis.

- A "Can Do" Optimistic Attitude
- A Growth Mindset
- Confidence, Belief, and Self-Worth
- Positive Inner Dialog
- Positive Outer Dialog and Interactions
- Managing Perfectionism
- Applying Affirmations to Re-Trigger the Subconscious
- Visualizing Motivational Forces
- Maintaining a Positive Physiology
- Bringing an Enthusiastic Spirit Everywhere

In my experience, far too many gifted athletes don't thrive at the elite level because they lack a well-developed positive belief system.

My daughter started playing tennis seriously at the age of 10. Every lesson, every day, every week I said to her as we would pick up tennis balls "Sarah, you're going to be playing the US Open if you keep training like this! Way to go!" Sarah played her first US Open at 15 years of age. Developing the personality traits of a champion doesn't replace training, it enhances it. At crunch time, it's all about the athlete's inner dialog. They're going to convince themselves that they can or can't, and either way, they're usually right.

At tournament sites, I routinely listen to the parent's dialog after the loss of their junior competitor. "You had'em again Kelly... you blew it." Well, guess what Kelly's new inner dialog is in future tight matches? "Come on... please don't blow it again...you always blow it!" While poor parenting sent the initial message, Kelly is now both the sender and receiver of this ongoing, catastrophic message. Breaking this cycle of a negative inner dialog is life changing. A key component in peak performance is a positive inner dialog.

It is worth repeating, that when it comes to self-coaching in competition, every athlete has a choice in dialog, to be self-encouraging or to be self-defeating. Far too often I witness athletes surprised that they're encountering hardships in tournament play. Thriving in competition is all about one's ability to expect hardships versus being surprised by it and of course, choosing a healthy response system.

> *"Positive personality traits program productive solutions. Negative personality traits produce unproductive excuses."*

The good news is that even if an athlete has programmed negative belief systems from early adolescence, it can be changed. Well-informed parents and coaches are typically the most influential adult figures and are positioned to help quiet the athlete's inner critic. Our daily messages become their inner voice.

For the technical coaching guru's reading this, I get it. If an athlete has no forehand, backhand, serve or volley but a great attitude, they're just going to be a happy loser. I'm not suggesting to train the athlete's software instead of their hardware; I'm saying train the software along with the hardware to maximize potential and increase competitive dominance.

CHAPTER 17: Building Coachable Athletes

During a seminar, I conducted at The Wingate Sports Institute in Tel Aviv, Israel an attending woman's volleyball coach raised her hand and asked me a great question: How does one discover their true potential? I responded, whether you're coaching, parenting or playing your chosen sport, realize that you're only one decision away from going up a level. The choice to avoid risk is what holds most of us back. Even before we attempt an endeavor, fear of the unknown forces most of us to retreat our efforts.

In psychology, it's called the Spotlight Effect. The brain hesitates when it perceives there's going to be a problem. We are hardwired to avoid pain and hardship whether it be physical, mental or emotional. It's easy to slide back and continue the same old comfortable routines, but "easy" only produces average results. Tennis coaches and players habitually choose to groove another basket of balls versus shifting their focus to the actual needs of the player (cause of losses). Why? It's far less painful.

What's holding us back is changing our decisions to taking risks versus routinely avoiding risks. Unpredictability and uncertainty should be seen as positive gatekeepers. I recommend moving towards those feelings versus running away from them. We all have an affinity for our habits. All too often we stay too long with those habits not because they're productive but because we're loyal to them.

A new relationship to anything may appear risky, but truth be told, it's often riskier to remain in an ineffective environment. The real danger lies in stagnation. We instinctively know that around the world, opponents are training smarter, faster and more efficiently. Remaining in our comfort zone will only leave us behind the competition. To our detriment, our brains will try to sabotage any and all attempts at doing anything uncomfortable. I recommend shifting focus from the negative attitude of "what could go wrong" to the positive attitude of "what could go right."

Whose responsibility is it to teach coach-ability? The typical response from a parent is, "I assume my child's coaches are teaching life skills…right?" Ask a coach and the response is, "Teaching life skills are the responsibility of the parents. They're paying me to teach their child strokes." Ideally, these core values are the result of everyone involved in the athlete's development, with the parents playing the decisive role. Providing children with the opportunity to take responsibility and instill accountability at an early age is not only an essential skill set for coach-ability but a vital life skill. Communication and independent problem-solving skills are the foundations of coach-ability.

"Two core software skills champions need most are millisecond decision making and problem-solving skills. Both of which, are not commonly found in standardized drilling."

Is Your Athlete Un-Coachable?

A gifted but un-coachable athlete is every coach's nightmare. The un-coachable athlete displays the following symptoms: showing up late for practice and lacking personal commitment, passion and real effort. These athletes routinely play the blame game, roll their eyes at constructive feedback and are close-minded to improvement. Un-coachable athletes spend the majority of their training sessions defending their poor choices and creating drama.

"Some athletes cling desperately to bad form because they have spent years developing it."

Being committed to one's emotional development isn't a genetic predisposition, it is a learned behavior nurtured by intelligent parents and coaches. Changing a talented yet un-coachable athlete into a coachable athlete takes great emotional aptitude from both the parents and coach.

Improving an athlete's software (coach-ability) is often a prerequisite for real learning, quicker growth, and maximizing potential. I believe great coaches and parents have to facilitate coach-ability. They have to convince the athlete that change is good, which is key because learning begins with change and change begins with learning.

Emotional modification begins with the athlete being open and honest enough to develop a humble and respectful attitude, competitive drive, and willingness to learn. It includes gratefulness that a coach cares enough and is willing to tackle the un-pleasantries of the task. Teaching discipline, accountability, and responsibility is a very different job description than teaching a topspin backhand.

Let's Look at the Characteristics of the Coachable Athlete:

- Willingness to Accept the Coach's Philosophy
- Acceptance of the Necessity for Improvement
- Desire to be Accountable
- Optimism and Growth Minded
- Respectfulness
- Acceptance of Responsibility
- Letting Go of Excuses
- Non-Combative Attitude
- Open-Minded too Constructive Criticism
- Eager to Receive Feedback

- Respectful of the Coach's Knowledge
- Selflessness
- Integrity
- Courageous

It's astounding how many young athletes self-sabotage their potential by choosing to ignore the above positive characteristics. Coachable athletes are taught life skills development and religiously held accountable for their morals and ethical conduct by their parents and coaches. Parents and athletes, please look for the above positive characteristics of the coachable athlete in your entourage of coaches as well. You can be sure that quality coaches will be looking for the same positive characteristics in their students and their parents.

In the 1st Edition of The Tennis Parents Bible (published in 2010), I wrote about the importance of positive coaching and parenting. A vital take away was the use of the 5-1 compliment to critique rule (verbal and non-verbal). If athletes are to fire their optimistic responses we have to provide the ammunition. I recommend exposing these qualities in timely condensed sessions. Coaches, the above 14 coachable software skills should be discussed in a creative, interactive information exchange that feels like a chat versus a moral lesson.

CHAPTER 18: Eliminating Internal Judgment

My neighbor, Pete, owns Pete's Home Repair Specialist. He's a super friendly independent contractor. Due to his excellent soft science personal skills, Pete's always in high demand. His decades of experience have taught him that detailed preparation prevents poor performance. Pete's truck is like an encyclopedia of tools organized by alphabet and ready for action. Though Pete doesn't need all of his tools at every job, he brings every tool, just in case he needs it.

This analogy is very similar to a high-performance tennis player's tool belt. In matches, they may not need to employ every skill set developed in their tool belt, but they do need to have primary and secondary strokes ready for competition, as well as multiple patterns and plays developed and prepared to be accessed if needed. Life skills, such as preparation improve the athlete's confidence, inner dialogue, and of course, solution-based self-coaching skills.

"In the heat of battle, the voice inside each athlete is their driving force."

In match play, an athlete's internal dialog is their self-coaching. Internal dialog is the conversation their ego is having with themselves. Athletes have a habitual way they choose to navigate their matches. When they see competition in a negative light, their internal dialog is dark. Conversely, when they "see pressure as a privilege," to quote Billy Jean King, their self-coaching is more positive, uplifting, and optimistic. The question is: Where did the athlete learn their internal dialog mantras?

An athlete's negative, problem-oriented inner dialog sabotages their performance by interfering with their quiet mind. To some athletes, negative inner dialog spirals them into a self-defeating, under-arousal state. To others, it pushes them into a panicked, over-arousal state. Both are detrimental to performance. As I mentioned earlier, an athlete's non-stop inner dialogue is either helping or hurting their performance. Intermediate athletes are known to sabotage their play by criticizing themselves, worrying about losing and inventing post-match catastrophic conclusions during competition.

How to Strengthen Self Coaching Solution#1:
Video Analysis

One method of combating the athlete's negative self-dialog begins with videotaping tournament matches and providing non-hitting match play video analysis. This process accesses the specific stressful environment that needs to be studied.

As the high IQ coach quantifies the match data alongside the athlete, I recommend identifying how the athlete's inner dialog helped or hurt their performance. Were they able to self-coach successfully? When providing match play analysis, remember to apply the five optimistic comments for every one pessimistic statement. Following are video analysis topics the athlete and coach would be wise to discuss.

Match Play Video Analysis

- Strokes & Movement Efficiencies & Deficiencies
- Anticipatory Efficiencies & Deficiencies
- Staying on Script. (Top 7 Patterns)
- Opponent Profiling
- Between Point & Change-Over Rituals & Routines
- Emotional Control

- Focus Control
- Cause of Errors
- Court Positioning Cause & Effect
- Score Management

Athletes who are trained to monitor their emotions and inner dialog via post-match video analysis are much more likely to become aware of the software complexities of competition.

How to Strengthen Self Coaching Solution #2:
Judgments through Comparisons

Judgmental thoughts typically stem from past or future thought comparisons. Typical thoughts of comparison in the heat of battle include, "Jason beat this dude. I can't lose, I've got to prove I'm better than Jason," "Kristin is ranked below me, and if I lose today, she'll take my spot on the team," "What are my parents and coaches going to say if I lose?" "Here I go...Choking again!"

Judgmental thoughts play havoc in the minds of our competitive athletes every day. Athletes in competition, with judgmental comparison thoughts, contaminate the match play process, which results in fighting two opponents, simultaneously- their negative thoughts and the real opponent.

Advanced athletes seeking better results often don't have to learn more technical skills; they have to shift their attention to developing better self-communication skills. Keep in mind that the athlete's inner voice will be with them long after they stop competing on the tennis court. Isn't it worth the time to assist them in developing their lifelong self-coaching tools? Winning is much more likely when our athletes understand the art of self-coaching.

How to Strengthen Self Coaching Solution # 3:
Positive Inner Dialog

The third method of conquering the athlete's negative inner dialog is through positive self-coaching with Neuro Priming. It is estimated that individuals have roughly 60,000 thoughts per day. Trading in a turbulent mental state for a relaxed, calming proactive state is essential.

What is Neuro Priming and why is it an essential addition to an athlete's preparation? Neuro Priming is the science of preprogramming the athlete's inner trust in their match solutions.

Mental rehearsals customize each athlete's positive inner dialog by organizing their physical, mental and emotional solutions into audio recordings in their voice. Listening to one's inner dialog audio tapes increases tennis IQ, reprograms old pessimistic beliefs, changes negative behaviors, speeds up the learning process, increases focus, assists the athletes in quickly fixing stroke flaws, staying on their script of patterns, coping with stress, nervousness and the fear of failure. Neuro Priming isn't meant to replace on-court physical training; its purpose is to enhance it. It's self-coaching at its best. *(Visit #1 Best Seller on Amazon: Neuro Priming for Peak Performance, Giampaolo).*

How to Strengthen Self Coaching Solution #4:
Identifying Internal Obstacles

Looking deeper into competitive success brings us to a fourth method, which is assisting athletes by identifying their internal obstacles. Although losing to a more experienced player stings a bit, losing to a toad because you have self-destructed is much more harrowing. The secret to conquering one's inner demons stems from understanding the importance of self-coaching. It is essential to master self-coaching with positive inner dialog by exchanging judgmental tirades with calming routines and rituals.

"Overcoming internal obstacles is more satisfying at a deeper level than beating a top seed."

Athletes perform best when they are not excessively judged or overly concerned about the outcome ramifications. Having outcome goals is fine, as long as their focus is on the process. To continually stay process-minded is the backbone of successful inner dialog. What influences athletes most in their toughest moments is their mental commentary. A healthy mindset orchestrates positive attitude, belief, and effort. So, what is competitive success? Competitive success is performing at one's peak performance level set after set; the optimum victory for any athlete.

How to Strengthen Self Coaching Solution #5:
Monitoring Outer Dialog

The fifth method of nurturing a positive inner dialog is to ask the athlete to monitor their outer dialog under stressful conditions. An athlete's outer dialog includes speech, body language, and physical behavior, which are natural bi-products of an athlete's internal dialog.

Monitoring this process begins with the athlete recognizing their automatic system of behavior under the stressful conditions of competition. Although it is common to default to old comfortable habits under stress; negative habits not only perpetuate pessimistic thought patterns, they alert the opponent that self-destruction is in the works. Self-spotting outer dialog behavior will help the athlete to recondition their inner dialog chatter.

How to Strengthen Self Coaching Solution #6:
Resist Attention Seeking Negative Dialog

A behavior management strategy is to coach the athlete to resist attention seeking negative dialog and behavior. Athletes gain sympathy by projecting pessimistic behaviors. A typical example of this is an athlete's excessively loud mini-tantrum in competition to gain sympathy from spectators, family or coaches. In essence, the athlete is projecting, "I'm usually so much better than this...I must be having an unusually bad day!" Ironically, the tantrum is seen every day.

In my opinion, tactically ignoring the outbursts in hopes that they go away is not dialog management because an appropriate alternate behavior is needed. An athlete's dialog projects their thoughts and beliefs. Their voices have been simply programmed into their subconscious. Since they determine the course of their life, reprogramming their negative inner chatter is a battle worth fighting.

"Optimistic self-coaching is a wonderful technique to create better human beings on and off the tennis court."

Here's an alternate view of tennis parenting and tennis teaching. The conventional method has been to feel balls, criticize what's broken and then focus on the athlete's problem areas. This judgment based approach isn't always in the student's best interest. Why? Because it subliminally plants the toxic seeds of negative inner dialog and in competition, this learned behavior of focusing on what's wrong opposes the natural flow state found in nonjudgmental, effortless, peak performance. Seeking "what is broken" isn't part of performing in the zone or "treeing" as today's juniors describe playing at one's optimal level.

CHAPTER 19: Changing Fixed Mindsets

Last week two top juniors, Steven and Josh were closing out one of their semi-private, two-hour sparring sessions. Josh from Boca Raton, Fl. has a natural inquisitive growth mindset. Steven, from San Francisco, California, possesses a defeatist attitude with his fixed mindset. Steven's a perfectionist and believes only perfect performances are acceptable.

As Steven was leaving Josh asked me if he could ask me a couple of questions. While I was packing up my gear, Josh asked, "Being solid at crunch time isn't something that just happens. It's something you have to develop, right?" "Absolutely," I replied. "Well, Steven's doesn't think he can win the whole Anaheim tournament next weekend, so he says he doesn't want to go. He'll probably fake an injury or something. His story is getting old. I don't understand why he puts so much pressure on himself to win. Even though I want to win every tournament I enter, I'm happy to play well. You know one point at a time. I hope to learn from my losses by working harder to improve. So by competing, I'm increasing my tennis intelligence and raising my level, right?"

I confirmed Josh's position and then said, "A growth mindset is about the journey of seeking mastery, instead of viewing losses as catastrophic. You can see losses as information gathering opportunities, and that buddy is why you're going to be famous!" Josh smiled, rolled his eyes and said "Good talk coach…good talk."

We've all had students who have high IQ's (Intelligence Quotient) but low EQ's (Emotional Quotient). These athletes are wired to avoid risk while they witness others thrive in competition.

A challenge within *The Soft Science of Tennis* is to educate these students that their mindset is only their perception of their abilities. After the athlete's stroke development is said and done, it's their optimistic or pessimistic attitude that determines competitive success on the tennis court. It is within the parent and coaches job description to develop the power of belief along with a powerful forehand.

Fixed Mindset individuals innately believe that their abilities are inborn and unchangeable.

Growth Mindset individuals trust that their skill sets can and will be developed and improved.

In my observations, fixed mindset students are typically overly sensitive to being wrong. They see failing in competition as catastrophic. If they lose, it's often something or someone else's fault, and constructive criticism is taken as a personal insult. Changing this mindset is one of the most challenging roles of a parent or coach.

Recognize the Negative Dialog

Athletes with a pessimistic viewpoint have a running dialog that continually persuades them that they don't honestly have enough talent, and if they fail, they will be criticized for trying. Many athletes invent an excuse or injury and avoid competition. By doing so, they keep their dignity and ego in check.

The following two solutions will help challenge the fixed mindset worrywart to consider adopting a growth mindset warrior attitude.

1. Explain that Mindset Is a Choice

Their mental habit is to choose to interpret competition as a serious personal threat. Fixed mindset athletes are typically worried about what could and will go wrong versus what could and will go right. This pessimistic view tears down the will to give 100% effort. Changing from the fixed mindset to the growth mindset is challenging because the athlete has an onslaught of two simultaneous opposing demands. One is the need to suppress their pre-set, negative mental habit and two is to be open to learning to embrace the exact opposite viewpoint.

2. Present the Opposing View

Fixed-mindset athletes need to be reminded that improving and growing requires a metamorphosis into a growth mindset. As these students ramp into tournament mode, be on high alert for their worry, stress, and fears to multiply. They view tournament competition as an event that will expose their shortcomings. It's our job to present tournament play as a healthy way to assess their development necessary to obtain their goals.

Warning: Responding to and changing their negative banter is emotionally draining even for the well-equipped software developing coach.

Examples of a fixed mindset approach include:

Athlete: "I can't play, my games not perfect yet. I'm not ready."

Teacher: "Every time you compete, you learn and improve, and that is the goal."

Athlete: "If I don't compete I won't fail, and I can keep my pride."

Teacher: "The only true failure is being too scared to try."

Training the stroke components is only the beginning of a world-class coach's journey. Having the tools to develop the whole athlete is the end game.

3. Religiously Spot the Positive

On practice days, I recommend applying the laws of attraction. Destroy their pessimistic point of view by asking them to say "yes" after performing a desired stroke or pattern of play. By doing so, it brings to light just how many good strokes they actually hit. This exercise combats their mental habit of focusing on the negative. Success starts by focusing on successes versus failures. It requires changing their doubt in their abilities because their doubt directly undermines their progress.

Once these pessimists see the progress in their abilities, they begin to show positive character traits and critical newborn life skills.

4. Commit to Playing One Game

On match days, fixed mindset "red flags" are everywhere as they try desperately to self-sabotage their performance. By doing so, they're building their arsenal of excuses for their ego out. "I would have won, but I didn't have time to train." "I could have won if I didn't have this blister on my thumb."

Also, typical with fixed mindset athletes is to try desperately to back out of competition the morning of the match.

The negotiation tactic I recommend is to ask them to enjoy their pre-match preparation and commit to playing at least one game. If the athlete still wants to default out after one game, that's fine. Once in the match, they almost always see that the environment is not as threatening as they perceived. The opponent's not as good as they imagined. So they play a few more games.

Teach my growth mindset philosophy: You have to be present to win. Opportunities and incredible victories present themselves if the athletes are willing to try.

Benefits of Competition for Fixed Mindsets

Many undeniable, positive aspects stem from tournament competition. Advantages include:

- Competition keeps us honest: It allows us to assess our strokes and movement efficiencies and deficiencies. Exposing our strengths and hiding our weaknesses is an important function of match play.
- Competition assists us in the art of opponent profiling. Without match play, there's no dissecting because there are no opponents.
- Competition exposes our mental fortitude. The ability to stay on Script (your customized game plan), strategy and tactics the match demands.
- Competition through failure and success helps us develop a massive list of life skills, positive character traits, and a moral compass.
- Competition aids in developing consistent quality. Winning a 64 draw event requires peak performance for approximately 15 sets.
- Competition assists us in customizing our future developmental schedules. It's not the quantity of on-court time; it's the quality that counts.

Tennis mastery is a process of continuous adaptation and improvement, which is a growth mindset system.

CHAPTER 20: Managing Fear and Risk

I've been a high-performance tennis coach for over 30 years. I thrived comfortably in relative obscurity, enjoying the Southern California sun working with nationally ranked junior tennis players and coaching coaches. For 20 of those years, I secretly dreamt of writing my own tennis instructional books to positively impact the coaching industry while traveling the world.

Procrastination dominated those 20 years. I wasn't willing to take the chance. I lacked the courage to risk leaving my base and losing my successful coaching business if I were to begin traveling. It seemed too dangerous. What if I failed? What if the books bombed? What if I wasn't as smart as I thought?

My internal dialog was telling me that even though I had something special to share, I shouldn't risk a good thing. I didn't have professional speaking experience. Why did I think I could write books?

I intuitively knew that I had to risk leaving relative comfort behind and put my old career in jeopardy in order to attract a larger audience and share my experiences and tennis developmental theories. I researched the fear and risk management process and began writing The Tennis Parents Bible. My goal was simply to complete it and if it helped a single parent or coach along their journey that would be a bonus.

Back then, no one could have told me I would go on to write four, #1 bestsellers, coach the ITF coaches and speak at the largest conferences and grand slams around the world.

Athletes respond to risk and fear differently. In my experience, while most athletes are initially overly cautious, some are overly adventurous. Success and failure in competition greatly depend on how the athlete responds to fear and risk. Results, both positive and negative, stem from repeated behavior. An athlete's behavior is created by their attitude. Therefore, understanding and managing our athlete's attitude toward fear and risk is worth exploring.

A great place to start when managing an athlete's attitude is establishing a baseline of their thoughts and behaviors concerning the following common stumbling blocks. Begin by answering the following question:

A. Do they have an adversity towards fear and risk? Is it extreme or mild?
B. Are they tolerant towards fear and risk?
C. Do they seek out fearful or risky endeavors? Is it extreme or mild?

Athletes possess different degrees of fear and risk depending on the conditions. For example, in competition, one athlete may exhibit extreme tolerance and grit while playing tennis behind the baseline and extreme adversity and fear when attacking the net. Other athletes may excel on the practice court displaying almost flawless stroke production only to shut down, choke or panic in competition. At the other end of the spectrum, some athletes possess no fear and live for the thrill of competition.

"Some extreme athletes hold only mild fear as they seek canoeing over Niagara Falls or bungee jumping over the Bhote Kosi River."

Most coaches hope that their athlete's strokes and athleticism have authority and command over their performance, but I believe it's their emotional aptitude that actually runs the show.

When working with players who have issues with fear and risk, begin by asking yourself the following six questions to identify the athlete's level of emotional awareness.

1) What is their cognitive design? Do they understand their brain preferences?
2) How do they view the feared situation?
3) Do they appreciate the opportunity to be able to compete?
4) Are there past bias or experiences they need to let go?
5) Will they accept a strategic, proactive plan to attack their issues?
6) Are they willing to train correctly for the mission at hand?

Conquering Fear Stems from a Courageous Plan

A re-occurring message throughout the book is that teaching tennis requires more than teaching the fundamentals of the game. It takes serious interpersonal skills. One necessary interpersonal skill is motivating athletes to dig deeper, push a little harder, and dare to compete in the face of fear. Courage is the ability to persevere and withstand fear. Unfortunately, in match play, fear often dismantles athletic performance.

"Peak Performance happens only when fear doesn't interfere with the process."

On the practice court when there's no real threat of negative judgment fear is minimal. Fear comes to life, in all its raging glory, when the athlete is judged during competition. In the competitive tennis world, fear is emotionally induced by a perceived threat, which is natural. Fear is real and best not to be ignored or treated lightly. Fear changes an athlete's brain chemistry, upsets the stomach, tenses muscle groups, and directly alters the athlete's behavior. So I'll say it again, fear is real and emotional training shouldn't be ignored.

When fear is interfering with performance, experienced competitors are trained to fight despite the perceived threat. While intermediate competitors, uneducated about the process, tend to freeze or cave into the pressure. I believe that the best way to conquer performance anxieties, such as fear, is to accept that they come with the privilege of competing.

Parents and coaches, simply telling an athlete not to be scared aren't preparing them for the onslaught of mental or emotional contaminants that will hold them hostage in match play. Overcoming debilitating fear comes from re-routing the athlete's brain. This entails shifting their focus away from the outcome of the match and toward their preset performance goals. Sounds easy, right? Wrong! Modifying the brains response to fear has to do with neuroplasticity. Eliminating the strong-lasting inner connections formed by poor mental habits takes time, thought, and daily effort.

Neuroscientists call this pruning. The process of pruning is unlearning by re-routing old, undesirable neural pathways, which form physical, mental or emotional barriers. For example, relax and cross your arms...no really! No one's looking. Cross your arms in a relaxed state. Now, consciously unwrap your arms and re-cross them the other way. Boom! It doesn't feel right, does it? This new motor program feels a bit uncomfortable and awkward. The same concept holds true after your spouse re-organizes the kitchen drawers and for two weeks you habitually go to the old spoon drawer only to find dish towels. As the new neuropathways are strengthened, the old pathways are weakened. It is a two-step system: Part one is pruning of the old mental habit, and part two is developing the new mental habit.

Uncle Tommy is 83 years young. In his home, he is kind, relaxed, funny and comfortable to be around. We hang out, watching Blue Blood re-runs and snack on junk food. But when we jump into his 2002 Camry (which we nicknamed "La Bomba") Uncle Tommy turns the key, and the different environment changes his brains chemistry, his attitude, and his body language. Within minutes, he's agitated, tense and uncomfortable.

Behind the wheel, Uncle Tommy feels a lack of control. He associates driving with uncontrollable reckless drivers, bumper to bumper traffic, and mayhem, which translates, to fear and risk. When a driver changes lanes without their blinker, Uncle Tommy's automatic response is to roll down the window and curse them out. I asked my wife if Tommy's emotional climate changes every time he drives his car? "Oh yah…every time. It's embarrassing!" Without re-wiring his agitated head space every time he sits behind the wheel he is strengthening that neural pathway and cementing his emotional response.

Conquering Fear through Desensitization

Let's use the analogy of Uncle Tommy's negative association with navigating "La Bomb" through the streets of Los Angeles with a tennis player who has a negative association with navigating tournament competition.

Like Uncle Tommy, some tennis player's brains chemistry changes for the worst as they prepare for competition. Their attitude and behavior flip due to their pre-set emotional response to fear and risk.

Whether it's fear of other drivers or fear of a competitor, disconnecting performance anxieties takes desensitization. This is an ongoing process of exposing the athlete to stress-busting, fear-based drills. These fear busting exercises replicate and expose the athlete to simulated versions of the emotional climate of competition.

The desensitization drills are followed by dress-rehearsal practice sets where pre-set, customized rituals and routines are in place. This pulls the athlete's attention toward the process instead of the outcome. Repeated exposure diminishes the stronghold anxiety has on the athlete. In sports psychology, they describe it as shifting focus from the "destructive neuropathway to the new enlightened neuropathway."

By learning and rehearsing a pro-active emotional response to fear, athletes (and even old uncles) can discover that their old belief system was merely a bad habit that formerly held them hostage.

Re-Examining Risk

Neuroscience shows us that it is normal human behavior to focus on what we could lose versus what we could gain. That is why some intermediate athletes play to win, get a comfortable lead then shift to playing not to lose, only to blow the lead. Their focus on avoiding possible pain causes probable pain.

When an athlete no longer fears losing, they embrace risk and play to win until the match is over. With this mindset, competition isn't threatening. The challenge is seen as a privilege.

Coaches and parents would be wise to remind their athletes that it is common for many athletes to be unknowingly loyal to comfortable mediocrity. Most want to fit in and not stand out. They prefer to protect the status quo and aren't willing to break their routines that are not working anyway. It's important for the educators to frequently motivate their athletes to remember that winning more often stems from improving, and improving comes from growing, and growing comes from risk. It is the internal challenge every competitive athlete faces.

The Risk Leads to Reward Philosophy

It's also important for us as parents and teachers to emphasize to our athletes that risk is inherent in competition. There are reckless risks, and then there are thoughtful, calculated, and inspired risks necessary to beat worthy opponents. Not all necessary risks pay off instantly. Sometimes risk initially leads to losses. Especially when the risky behavior (pattern play, shot selection or stroke) hasn't been fully developed. When your student attempts the correct shots the moment demands, whether they win or lose, they are improving their mastery of the sport.

"Without appropriate risk-taking, nothing new would ever be accomplished."

In beginner and intermediate tennis competition, playing it safe and retrieving often pays great dividends. However, in high-performance tennis, it's a different story. At the higher levels, playing it safe and not taking advantage of appropriate risks is usually a receipt for failure. Without pushing your athletes to embrace risk, they will likely remain stagnant in their growth and predictable in their match play. Athletes who embrace risk are more likely to realize their true potential.

> **"Athletes have to risk defeat, judgment, pain, and shame to play at their peak potential.**

Taking intelligent risks is an essential part of achieving high-performance tennis results.

Managing Risky Players

Like we uncovered in previous chapters, not all athletes share the same cognitive profile. We are all controlled to some extent by our genetic design. While parents and coaches promote the rewards of taking calculated risks to some athletes, it is wise to understand that other cognitive designs need polar opposite training. To these, reckless daredevils, minimizing risk is in their best interest. Some of our athletes aren't thinking of reasons not to risk; they are thinking why not risk…

Opposite of the timid performers are the reckless athletes who are hard-wired to thrive on risk. In fact, they perform with too much reckless abandon. They are often downright mindless and inattentive to playing high percentage ball. This

162

personality profile doesn't have limiting beliefs; they have limitless beliefs.

I occasionally work with talented, young juniors who are so overly confident that they are sure they're going to be #1 in the world next week! Due to their limitless beliefs, nothing is stopping them from routinely attempting low percentage shot selections. Their intuition is skewed, as we watch in horror as these impatient athletes give away relatively easy matches.

With these exciting athletes, I recommend assisting them to play only within their pre-set comfortable script of play. Firstly, assist them in designing their most proficient serving patterns, return patterns, rally patterns, short ball options, and net rushing sequences. Second, practice these exact scripts routinely in place of rallying. Third, bring in a sparring partner and monitor the athlete's ability to stay on their pre-designed scripts throughout practice sets. Forth, in real tournament play, chart the percentage of points the athlete played on script versus going rogue. In my experience, exceptions follow every rule so shoot for a performance goal consisting of about 75% on script and 25% off script. The athletes should seek excellence and not perfection.

> *"Champions understand that if they don't apply intelligent risk, they don't grow. If they don't grow, they don't reach their peak potential. If they aren't performing at their peak potential, they're not satisfied with their performance. If they're not satisfied, they're not happy. So, happiness stems from risking intelligently."*

CHAPTER 21: Developing Confidence and Self Esteem

Bill is a 6 foot lanky 14-year-old who is top 15 in Southern California. Tennis has come very easy to Bill. He is naturally athletic and much taller than his peers. Bill and his folks are convinced he's on track to becoming an ATP Professional. He attends a local Tennis Academy, where he hits for 4 hours a day on the practice court, playing "catch" back and forth. He is also one of the best juniors at the academy.

Bill's fundamental strokes are dynamite. He walks on-court cocky, smiling, and confident. During tournaments, however, when matches flip 180 degrees to a game of "keep away" Bill misses a few shots, begins to panic and turns into a completely different person. His verbal outbursts are self-belittling, and his body language and facial expressions are borderline crazy as tear roll down his cheeks.

After reviewing with Bill one of his so-called catastrophic losses, I asked him, "What are your thoughts about your performance?" Bill stated, "I played awful! I am so confused because I beat everyone in practice games, but in real tournament matches, if I miss an easy shot, I freak out and lose all belief. Man, I have no confidence in tough matches. Sometimes I get so upset that I can't even find my strings and I turn into shank-zilla. What is wrong with me?"

If strokes and athleticism are the muscles and bones of the athlete, confidence and self-esteem are the heart and soul. Let's go back in time and review the origins of the words: confidence and esteem.

In Latin, the word confidence means to trust. Self-confidence refers to the athlete's inner-emotional ability. It's their opinion of their aptitude to engage and compete successfully.

A self-confident person is eager to take on challenges and seeks new opportunities.

In Latin, the word esteem means to appraise. Self-esteem refers to the athlete's inner emotional view of their self-worth. Athletes with high self-esteem feel secure, confident, and worthwhile.

Nurtured self-confidence and self-esteem typically precede any real athletic accomplishments. Without these soft science skills, athletes often hold themselves back by inaction due to fear and uncertainties. The majorities of athletes do not include emotional training in their tennis development and are not nurtured how to believe in themselves. As a result, emotionally weak competitors often view competition as a high-risk activity instead of an opportunity.

Some players have tremendous athletic skills but don't trust their abilities.

Performing at one's peak potential in practice is easy because the athletes are not keeping real score so they are aren't being judged. In tournament competition, judgment is inherent. Once the umpire calls out "LETS PLAY," mental and emotional fear-based interferences come into view.

Do you ever wonder why some athletes stand up and fight at crunch time, routinely seizing the moment, while others wilt due to self-doubt and lack of courage? The difference lies in their inner belief, confidence, self-trust, and self-esteem.

The following is a list of open-ended questions that will assist in assessing the underlying confidence and self-esteem within your athlete.

- Can peak performance coexist with having fun?
- If you're focusing exclusively on your shortcomings, how does it help? Could it hurt?
- If you focused on solutions, how could that help?
- What is confidence?
- What does self-esteem have to do with your inner dialog?
- Why does practice in the manner you're expected to perform make sense?
- What is needed to compete more confidently and comfortably?
- Are you willing to be uncomfortable in practice in order to be comfortable in matches?
- In competition, what is uncomfortable to you?
- Are you ready to push past your walls and test your limits?
- Where does mediocre training lead?
- What poor, unproductive choices can you turn down?
- Gamesmanship requires confrontation. How are you prepared to conquer your inner demons and then fight for your rights?
- How do you accept feeling fearful but focus and stay on script anyway?
- Why does healthy self-confidence lead to successful experiences?
- How do successful experiences lead to increased confidence?

Memories are Malleable

Over time, the mental images of an event shape one's view of the situation and memories are created. We choose which "past movie" runs in our minds. With events like weddings, we forget the bad (Aunt Martha got up and sang "Feelings" with the band) and recall the good (Dad cried through the entire ceremony.)

In regards to athletic competition, we tend to do the polar opposite. We forget the good and magnify the bad. Frequently, over-zealous parents go to great lengths to document detailed laundry lists of their athlete's match performance shortcomings and then proceed to review their findings with their athlete right after the match, which of course, disheartens the athlete. With persistent criticism, the athlete begins to build a subconscious, un-penetrable wall of memory recounting their failures. Confidence or lack thereof is malleable like our memory.

Reinforcing the behaviors you seek versus pointing out failures is in the athlete's best interest. If your athletes can benefit from increased confidence, check out the following five solutions.

Starting a Brand New Memory System

1. **Ask the athlete to inventory their well-developed competitive tool belt.**

These include life skills, positive character traits, morals, various game styles, primary strokes, secondary strokes, match day routines and rituals, mental skills, emotional skills, self-destruction skills, etc. These well-developed tools are convincing reasons to be confident.

2. **Ask the athlete to complete a success journal.**

They do so by going online and reviewing their positive tournament match success stories from the past few years. Re-living scenarios where they overcame hardship, conquered gamesmanship, performed at their peak performance level, stayed on script for the duration of the match, improved their statistical numbers, handled poor conditions, beat that pusher, took out a top seed, or won a title. These past success stories are incredibly motivational as they provide the leverage the athlete needs to build their inner trust. These accomplishments are significant, influential memories to journal and re-live.

3. **After a solid performance, ask the athlete to write a congratulations letter to them self.**

Have them list in detail all the success in the four main components- strokes, athleticism, mental and emotional. Such as their strong strokes, their outstanding athleticism, their rock-solid strategies, as well as their triumphant emotional state. Ask them to reread the letter before matches and after losses. There are enough people in the world that will tell them that they can't do it. Athletes don't need themselves promoting the negative.

4. **Ask the athlete to complete a "life" gratitude checklist.**

It's almost impossible to continually focus on negative issues such as disappointments, problems, stress, and fear while simultaneously highlighting successes, positive attributes, and opportunities. Examples range from getting to play tennis, traveling to tournaments, owning the latest clothes and gear, eating well, sleeping well, loving pets, great friends, loving family and of course, their supportive coaches.

5. **Ask the athlete to design a brand new customized developmental plan.**

Belief follows quality persistent, repetitive practicing in the manner they're expected to perform. This training methodology is very different than hitting another basket of balls. An individual's belief only changes after their routines change. Studies show that the athlete's actual biochemistry changes if and when the athlete is willing to change their approach. New habits should become the athlete's new focal point.

Make time to assist the athlete in writing down their five newly adapted memory systems. Encourage the athlete to record the appropriate memories into their cellular phone's digital recorder app and listen to their brand new memory system nightly to help reinforce their new improved confidence and self-esteem.

Destroying old bad habits, technical, mental or emotional, is not a one-time fix. Re-programming skills and thought processes demand repetition. Confidence and self-esteem are mastered through daily exercises. Changing their memory system leads to increased self-confidence, which leads to successful experiences, and these successful experiences lead to even greater confidence. It becomes a powerful upward spiral that every athlete, parent, or coach seeks.

CONCLUSION

It is my hopes that *The Soft Science of Tennis* reveals insights that motivate parents and coaches to create an irresistible, positive culture. This book highlights why there's more to developing a champion that meets the eye and how specific educational pathways should be customized to suit the sixteen different personality profiles found within your students.

The heart of *The Soft Science of Tennis* recognizes brain preferences and why it's an essential tool which enables us to maximize athletic potential at a much quicker rate. The values and beliefs shared throughout these pages define how coaches and parents will connect with their athletes at a deeper level in the very near future.

The soft science concept is a new way of looking at things for many industry professionals. Rather than continuing to place exclusive emphasis on fundamental stroke perfection, the focus is now on the whole athlete. Developing the athlete's software (mental and emotional) is just as significant as developing their hardware (strokes and athleticism.)

Connecting with someone shouldn't have to feel like winning the lottery. It should be an everyday experience. To me, coaching is never just about the drill. I care much more about how people feel when they're improving. That's the real connection. The emotional connection between people is the real magic. In writing this book, it's my wish that coaches and parents apply these insights to establish a genuine bond with their athletes and connect on a higher level.

Enjoy the journey, Frank

TESTIMONIALS FROM THE INTERNATIONAL TENNIS INDUSTRY

"This is an absolute must read book for all coaches and professionals. Frank really knows his stuff!"

Allistair McCaw, *Ft Lauderdale, Florida, World renowned sports performance and mindset coach, speaker, and author.*

"*The Soft Science of Tennis* is filled with golden nuggets of wisdom that can be implemented to achieve peak performance on and off the court. As a high-performance coach, I am fascinated and downright obsessed with helping players, parents, and coaches. This book is a game changer! Frank has done a masterful job of going deep into the how communication, self-talk, and understanding personality types impact performance. I strongly recommend *The Soft Science of Tennis* to anyone interested in going to the next level."

Jeff Salzenstein, *Denver Colorado, Founder of Tennis Evolution, Former Top 100 ATP Singles And Doubles Player, Stanford All-American, USTA High Performance Coach, and co-creator of The Connection Game*

"I recommend that every USPTA and PTR professional should read this book. It will help them be more successful in their business and personal life. I am going to have all my pros read it. Thanks Frank for making our industry grow!"

Doug Cash, *Seymour, Indiana Cashflowtennis*

"Frank Giampaolo's ability to share his real-world tennis experience provides coaches and parents a toolbox for Effective Communication! *The Soft Science of Tennis* provides a practical Game Plan to help our athletes. Problems are identified; their causes isolated and specific Action Steps recommended. Who could ask for more?"

Dr. Bryce Young, *Hilton Head South Carolina co-author of The Courtside Coach: A Personal Mental Trainer for Tennis Players and Mental Coach for 300 university teams*

"Frank is in front of his time as a coach. By writing a book dedicated to the soft skills of being a tennis coach, Frank demonstrates his enormous experience and understanding of what it truly takes to be an extraordinary coach. The soft skills are without a doubt a neglected area of coaching that is essential to the effectiveness of coaching. In this book, Frank dissects the area and provides an easy to understand framework of how you can better your soft skills."

Adam Blicher, *Odense, Denmark, Sports Psychology Consultant, Awarded Coach of the year, Danish National coach, Host of the highest rated Tennis Coaches Podcast on iTunes.*

"*This Soft Science of Tennis* offers the breakthrough moments when age-old questions become answers. Frank shows why software development is just as important as the development of the athlete's hardware. This is a highly recommended read for all tennis professionals."

Joe Dinoffer, *Dallas, Texas PTR and USPTA Master Professional and Founder of OnCourt OffCourt.*

"Frank has definitely hit the nail on the head in his new book *The Soft Science of Tennis*. This book is a must-read for all coaches looking to truly connect with their athletes, with additional tools to help coaches understand the impact of athlete-centered coaching philosophy. With every turn, of the page, you are immersed in resources to develop stronger competitors, but most importantly, software that will help your athletes become successful in life."

Brian Parkkonen, *Orlando, Florida, PTR Director of Education*

"I love that Frank covers proper communication in his new book: *The Soft Science of Tennis* and the importance it plays in performance. He writes about how a coach's communication impacts a child's confidence levels, inside and outside of tennis. Frank touches on some key aspects - developing the ability to ask good open-ended questions and listen to a child's response. This allows kids to become an empowered part of the decision-making process impacting their tennis playing and life."

Dr. Michelle Cleere, *Oakland, California Elite Performance Expert*

"Great tennis books continue to flow from the pen of Frank Giampaolo. His latest book *The Soft Science of Tennis* is yet another outstanding book that any student of the game--player, coach or parent--should make it a point to read and digest. This book is going to occupy pride of place in my home library."

Dr. Desmond Oon, *Long Beach, California Performance Psychologist, Zen Master, Master Professional, USPTA*

"Frank has hit another 'ace' with his latest book The Soft Science of Tennis. He is a wealth of information in so many areas of tennis and always does a fantastic job in addressing the needs of athletes, parents and coaches. This book's an amazing read touching on the hidden topics of advanced communication and personality profiling which are often missed by many coaches."

Michele Krause, Sarasota, Florida TIA Global Education Director- Cardio Tennis

"The Soft Side of Tennis is filled with insight and inspiration to help you reach your potential. In this extraordinary book, Frank Giampaolo shows you how to successfully utilize your skill set by developing a positive mindset."

Roger Crawford, Sacramento California, Host of Tennis Channel's Motivational Monday's, Best-Selling Author-Hall of Fame Speaker

"Ground Breaking! The 'In the Trenches' research, wisdom, and inspiration are becoming Franks trademarks. As a fellow trench pro for 40 years using the court as a laboratory, I believe it's the job of the coach to get in the world of the student not the student getting into the world of the coach. *The Soft Science of Tennis* will change the way you look at yourself, your loved ones, and your students forever."

Angel Lopez , Director of Tennis/Head Tennis Professional, San Diego Tennis and Racquet Club/Angel Lopez Tennis Academy

"Communication is at the center of a healthy parent-child and athlete-coach relationship. Sadly, many parents and coaches aren't the best communicators. In Frank's latest book, he gives concrete evidence and advice to both parents and coaches so they can do a better job interacting with their developing players. Frank is a regular on the ParentingAces Podcast - our audience loves his brutal honesty and no-nonsense approach to helping athletes develop to their full potential. *The Soft Science of Tennis* is one more valuable addition to any Tennis Parent's home library."

Lisa Stone, *Atlanta, Georgia Owner, ParentingAces*

"Coaches and Parents will love Frank Giampaolo's *The Soft Science of Tennis*! Frank provides a clear picture of how to work with athletes from the player's perspective and learning style. He discusses Mental and Emotional strategies that players need in order to perform on the court as well as in life. He, then, gives the reader strategies to implement them! Coaches and players will greatly benefit! If you want to take your players to the next level, I highly recommend *The Soft Science of Tennis*!"

Linda LeClaire, *Hilton Head, South Carolina, Energy Coach, Mental Coach, author of The Confidence Factor and Yes, God Speaks to Women, Too! A Message of Health, Healing and Hope*

"Well done Frank! Yet again you have written another wonderful and insightful body of work. By utilizing *The Soft Science of Tennis*, coaches, and parents will drive athletic performance, productivity, boost morale, and have greater impact on the athlete's results."

Neil Biddle, *United Kingdom, PTR Professional, Great Britain National tester, Director: The Tennis Coaches Network*

"For almost two decades, I've coached against Frank Giampaolo. In the last few years, I've had access to his publications and gained tremendous insight into his coaching mind. His most recent book, *The Soft Science of Tennis*, delves into the brain in ways that can make all coaches better. Knowing how our students learn is step one. Showing us how to approach these students with our information, Frank provides step two.

As a player, a larger toolbox means you are able to solve more problems on-court. In coaching, a larger toolbox means we have more approaches to transfer our information effectively. *The Soft Science of Tennis* is a chainsaw in the world of coaching artistry. With it, we can carve, sculpt and chisel away the unnecessary bark of our students and quickly get to the core of things. Kudos to Frank for taking time to step away from the court to transfer this wisdom to the parenting, coaching community."

Craig Cignarelli, *St. Petersburg, Florida, WTA Tour Coach*

"Frank Giampaolo has done it again... Just when you thought things couldn't get better, they have! *The Soft Science of Tennis* will truly impact the athletes, parents, and coaches. This is a book of wisdom, and Frank is passing this on with his usual energetic exuberance. I recommend this for club professionals, directors, parents and students. This is not just about tennis, it is about life, I say Well Done!"

Alec Horton, *Los Angeles, California Director of Tennis Operations, Griffin Club*

"Serious players know that tennis mirrors life. Great players train with that in mind. No one understands this better than Frank Giampaolo, who's pioneering insights about applying 'soft skills' on-court will undoubtedly bring out the best in players and coaches alike."

P.J. Simmons, *New York, New York Founder, The Tennis Congress*

"Franks latest book *The Soft Science of Tennis* is 100% the next book you must read! Communication is key, and Frank's ability to communicate in all the ways in which we can communicate better is outstanding in this book. It's easy and fun to read, and you will get hooked on his message."

Bill Riddle, *Nashville, Tennessee - PTR/ USPTA Elite Tennis Professional International Speaker/ Presenter*

"Frank has hit it out of the park again. I am lucky enough to know Frank personally, and I can say without reservation that he "gets it". Frank spends a great deal of effort listening to others. This is his trick to shaping his ideas and thoughts regarding the dissection of the inner workings of tennis players.

Once again, he has climbed deep into the weeds to explain a very important facet of our sport and our players that is the inner mental and emotional that most teaching professionals won't spend the time researching. This aspect is so critical to the success of players. I particularly love the story of how Frank came to the VBTC. I have heard him tell it me several times and it never gets old. Thanks Frank for another groundbreaking piece. Keep them coming."

Lane Evans, *Hendersonville, North Carolina, USPTA Southern President, USPTA Tester & National Fitness & Wellness Committee Chairman*

"Frank is a master at coaching tennis. What I absolutely love about him is his outside of the box thinking that makes you say, "Wow this is very interesting! *The Soft Science of Tennis* is another home run."

Monty Basnyat, *San Francisco Ca. Tennis Director, Certified Mental Toughness Specialist USTA High Performance Coach, US Professional Tennis Association - Elite Pro, Past President Norcal USPTA Division*

"*The Soft Science of Tennis* is a well-written book of powerful thoughts, ideas and ways for advancing athletes to the highest level! Solid progression and flow with each chapter starting at the beginning with Creating Exceptional Culture to Non-Verbal Communication to Personality Profiling and on and on!"

Mike Casey, *Cabo San Lucas, Mexico, Director of Tennis, Discovery Land Company, El Dorado Beach Club*

"*The Soft Science of Tennis* is the must-read book for any coach, parent, and player. As a coach, it helps you identify the areas that'll take you from good to great. The valuable insight shared through situational stories hits home on what coaches face daily with players. After reading this book, I saw immediate impact on my effectiveness as a coach creating a better environment for my players."

Susan F. Nardi, *Los Angeles, California, Director of Jr Tennis Griffin Club, PTR Tester, USPTA Elite Professional*

"*The Soft Science of Tennis* is a must read for coaches and players aspiring to achieve their full potential in tennis. The book is thoughtfully and skillfully written to help every player develop an understanding of the key emotional skills essential for optimum performance. Frank Giampaolo continues to deliver great work to the Tennis World in his latest book!"

John Craig, *Newport Beach, California, USPTA Division President, Performance Plus Tennis*

"Frank has such a gift for seeing and explaining how to work with athletes. *The Soft Science of Tennis* Makes a complicated methodology ingeniously simple."

Pat Whitworth, *Suwanee, Georgia USPTA Master Professional-Southern Executive Director*

"I'm sure Frank Giampaolo has another best seller on his hands with his new book: *The Soft Science of Tennis*. During my decades of coaching high school tennis, I suspected I wasn't the only coach who struggled with discovering the athlete's unique learning preferences. Congratulation to Frank! You have made the emotional and mental aspect of sports extremely accessible to coaches, parents, and players with this insightful new book, *The Soft Science of Tennis*."

John Danise, *Sebastian, Florida, PTR Professional, Executive Director FHSTCA, Past board member USTA*

FRANK GIAMPAOLO BIO

Frank Giampaolo is an award-winning coach, popular international speaker, and sports researcher. He is an instructional writer for ITF (International Tennis Federation) Coaching & Sports Science Review, UK Tennis magazine, the USPTA, Tennis Magazine, Tennis Pro Magazine and Tennis View Magazine. Frank is both a USPTA and PTR educator, a Tennis Congress Factuality Member, and has been a featured speaker at the Australian Grand Slam Coaches Convention, the PTR GB Wimbledon Conference, and Wingate Sports Institute (Israel.)

Frank is the bestselling author of Championship Tennis (Human Kinetics Publishing), Raising Athletic Royalty, The Tennis Parent's Bible (volumes I & II), Emotional Aptitude In Sports and Neuro Priming for Peak Performance. His television appearances include The NBC Today Show, OCN-World Team Tennis, Fox Sports, Tennis Canada and Tennis Australia.

Frank founded The Tennis Parents Workshops in 1998, conducting workshops across the United States, Mexico, Israel, New Zealand, Australia, England, Canada and Spain. Frank's commitment to coaching excellence helped develop over 100 National Champions, hundreds of NCAA athletes, numerous NCAA All-Americans and several professional athletes. His innovative approach has made him a worldwide leader in athletic-parental education. Frank is currently the Vice Chair of the USTA/SCTA Coaches Commission.

Contact Frank Giampaolo:
(949)933-8163
FGSA@earthlink.net
www.MaximizingTennisPotential.Com

SUGGESTED READING

Fairhurst A and Fairhurst (1995) Effective Teaching Effective Learning, Palo Alto, CA; Davies Black Publishing

Kiersey D(1988) Portraits of Temperament , California; Prometheus Nemesis

Lawrence G (1993). People Types and Tiger Stripes, The Centre for Applications of Psychological Type Inc.

Lawrence G (2005). Looking at Type and Learning Styles, The Centre for Applications of Psychological Type Inc.

Gardner, Howard (1999) Intelligence Reframed. Multiple Intelligences for the 21st century, New York: Basic Books. 292 + x pages. Useful review of Gardner's theory and discussion of issues and additions.

Murphy E (1993) The Developing Child: using Jungian Type to Understand Children, Paulo Alto, CA; Davies Black Publishing.

Quenk N L (2000) Essentials of the Myers Briggs Indicator Assessment, New York: Wiley (® MBTI and Myers-Briggs Type Indicator are registered trademarks of the Myers-Briggs Type Indicator Trust.)

Return to TOC

Made in the USA
Lexington, KY
20 November 2018